THE STUDY OF THE NEW TESTAMENT

THE STUDY OF THE NEW TESTAMENT

CLARENCE TUCKER CRAIG

ABINGDON PRESS
NEW YORK   NASHVILLE

THE STUDY OF THE NEW TESTAMENT

Copyright 1939 by Clarence Tucker Craig

Library of Congress Catalog Card Number: 39-11037

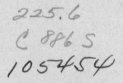
PRINTED AND BOUND AT NASHVILLE,
TENNESSEE, UNITED STATES OF AMERICA

CONTENTS

PREFACE

THIS brief Introduction to the New Testament has been written in the hope that it may help lay Christians attain a modern, historical understanding of the early Christian writings. It is designed for use in adult and young people's classes in the church school, for the guidance of pastors who wish to devote their midweek service to Bible study, and for a Leadership Training School text. If the Bible is to be read intelligently by Christian people, they must receive assistance in understanding the circumstances under which the books were written.

The chapters have been arranged for one quarter's study in the church school, or a unit of twelve lessons in a Leadership Training School. In the latter case the twelve chapters should be used, leaving the Introduction to be read by the students independently, and discussed in connection with Chapter Twelve. Since it is often customary to hold two sessions on the same evening, the chapters have been arranged in convenient pairs.

No attempt is made to study the books in the order in which they were written, for with the later books that is quite conjectural. John is treated before Luke so that the two volumes of Luke-Acts may be kept together. The latter then serves as an introduction to Paul. A disproportionate amount of space is given to the Epistle to the Hebrews and to Revelation, for it is believed that readers are less likely to study these books elsewhere. A separate course should be given to the Pauline message. The study of the Gospels does not aim to provide a brief life of Jesus or a survey of his teaching. The hope is, rather, that students may come to a truer evaluation of the sources of our information about Jesus.

A portion of this material appeared in *The Elementary Magazine* and acknowledgment is made of the privilege of reprinting it in this form.

INTRODUCTION

THE APPROACH TO THE NEW TESTAMENT

THE Bible has the widest circulation of any book in the world. But, as with all great books, it is not easy to understand; as with everything noble, it is in danger of misuse. If it is to serve the greatest good, it must be approached in a fruitful way. Not every key unlocks its truth. If anyone is to receive the greatest help from the Bible, he must follow an approach which will unfold its true message.

Throughout much of Protestant history there has been a *dogmatic approach* to the Bible. This stress arose to offset the Roman Catholic appeal to the authority of the Church. Men began with a particular theory of the inspiration of its pages. It was held that since this was the Word of God, it must be inerrant. There could be no essential differences in that which had been literally inspired by the Holy Spirit. From its pages a standard of conduct and belief was to be derived which was authoritative for the Church. It was true that as differing denominations appealed to the same "infallible book" they often arrived at quite different standards. Nevertheless, for many years the Bible was set apart from all other books by preconceived ideas of what revelation should mean.

If such a theory is no longer held so widely, it is not due to unbelief. Reverence for the truth makes it no longer possible to maintain this approach. Surely, there is no infallibility in *the selection* of the particular books of the Bible. The twenty-seven books comprising our New Testament were not finally deter-

mined until the fourth century. From the extant
records of the earliest Christians, those were chosen
which had been most valuable in the experience of
the Church. In the second century, 1 Clement and
the Shepherd of Hermas appeared much more likely
to be received into the canon than many of the books
which were finally approved. That the Fathers were
guided by the Holy Spirit in that selection we need
not doubt, but no modern scholar would agree that
they were inerrant when they included such a late
book as Second Peter.

Likewise, there can be no infallibility in *the text*.
In the copying of the New Testament manuscripts by
hand during the period of fourteen hundred years before the invention of printing, many variations arose.
Modern textual study has demonstrated that the King
James Version must be altered at many points in order
to agree with the best evidence for the original Greek.
But there is no infallibility in the judgment of the
scholars who pursue the painstaking study necessary
to restore that text. If an infallible text ever existed,
it is certainly not possible for us to recover it today.
This should not disturb any reader, for the number
of passages concerning which there is serious doubt is
relatively small; but it is fatal to any dogmatic theory.

Furthermore, there is no infallibility in *content*.
Unimportant matters will be chosen for illustration,
but no point could be inconsequential for a dogmatic
theory of inerrancy. Surely, there was only one inscription over the cross of Jesus, but no two Gospels
give exactly the same wording of that inscription.
Jesus died on a Friday, but Mark and John do not
agree as to what day of the month it was. Paul speaks
in 1 Corinthians 10. 8 of twenty-three thousand who

died in the wilderness, while the passage in Numbers 25. 9 speaks of twenty-four thousand. Obviously, no religious values are affected by such discrepancies, but they are decisive obstacles to dogmatic theories of inerrancy.

We believe in the inspiration of the Bible because a reading of its contents inspires us. We believe that the New Testament is revealed Scripture because it contains the earliest records of God's self-manifestation in Christ. We do not depend upon the belief that these books were written under entirely different circumstances than others. No author had any realization that he was producing a document which would find its place alongside of "Scripture," that is, the Old Testament. We must not start with preconceived notions concerning the contents of the Bible, but build up our ideas of inspiration and revelation from a careful study of the books themselves.

A second approach to the Bible is *the devotional*. Here the reader comes to the Bible with the sole aim of securing spiritual help. He is not concerned with what the author intended to say to the first readers. He simply asks, "What does this passage say to me?" There is no desire for exegetical, historical, or geographical helps. The only quest is for the illumination of the Holy Spirit to his own soul through the stimulus of the sacred page.

Though the dogmatic approach is definitely false, the devotional attitude toward the Bible will always have its place and value. Untold millions have received comfort and help from its pages who had no idea of the original circumstances under which they were written. Often they have read into the book quite different ideas from those which the original author held. But since the purpose of this approach is to receive inward strengthening, it does not seem important to them to distinguish between what comes from a literal reading of the printed page and what comes from the direct guidance of the Spirit of God. The devotional treasures of the Bible are great. There are probably many persons who will never be led to any other interest in the Bible than the reading of short passages, irrespective of context, which bring daily guidance and inspiration.

Nevertheless, there are perils in a purely devotional approach. Foremost is the peril of *allegorizing*. It has been a bane of Biblical study for centuries. When the literal meaning of a passage gives no satisfactory message, ingenious imagination has found a "spiritual" interpretation. Before the beginning of Christianity, Jews were already using allegory to explain parts of their Scriptures. Paul was trained in such methods. We have a perfect example when he contends that "Thou shalt not muzzle the ox when he treads out the corn" was really intended to teach that apostles should be supported by the community. The original humanitarian purpose is replaced by one akin to Paul's own interest. Some parts of the Bible were written as allegory and must be understood as such, but when we allegorize other passages, we read into the Bible our own ideas rather than submit to its guidance.

The devotional use of the Bible has its place as long as we recognize its nature. When words of Scripture give wings to our minds, we should be free to follow the leading of the Spirit. But we must never forget that a given passage of any book contains one definite meaning which the author was endeavoring to convey to his readers. Only exact methods of interpretation can arrive at that meaning. We should heed the warning of the author of Second Peter, "No prophecy of scripture is of private interpretation." No matter what differing intuitions various readers may receive, the only correct interpretation of a passage is one reached according to methods open to all.

A third approach to the Bible is *the literary*. We are often exhorted to read the Bible because it is a literary classic. Undoubtedly, the King James Version has been influential in molding English speech, and lovers of fine prose are delighted by its majestic cadences. Portions of Isaiah and Job rank among the greatest masterpieces in any language. No one can be considered truly educated who has not read widely in this collection of Hebrew and early Christian writings.

Nevertheless, the importance of this approach can be greatly overemphasized. A relatively small number of people are drawn to the reading of great literature. Considering the extent of world literature, few will return frequently to the Bible simply because of its literary merits. Certainly, the Christian Church does not owe its interest in the Bible to the literary value of some translation, but to the religious values which are in the original. There is other prose or poetry which twentieth-century men and women may well prefer for the sheer joy of reading.

Particularly with the New Testament is there reason to minimize the importance of the literary approach. The Old Testament does contain the greatest monuments of Hebrew literature, but few teachers of Greek would assign a passage in the New Testament simply for its literary value. The books which are included in our New Testament were not written by authors with literary pretentions. They were written by men without scholarly attainments, and much of what they wrote is very colloquial. There are passages in Paul of real eloquence, and the authors of both the Epistle to the Hebrews and the Gospel of Luke evidently had some literary ambitions. But on the whole we must say that the New Testament is great literature only in the sense that it has a theme of commanding importance. The original is clothed in the speech of the ordinary man.

Objection is sometimes raised against the new translations of the Bible because they have exchanged the sonorous periods of the King James Version for a more colloquial form of expression. As a matter of fact, that is necessary in order to be true to the originals. No Greek of the first century would ever have been attracted to the Gospel according to Mark for its literary value. It is doubtful if many Americans will in the twentieth century. The real claim to the importance of the New Testament must lie elsewhere.

A fourth approach to the Bible is *the historical*. Any sound endeavor to understand the Bible must start from this standpoint. It views the books of the New Testament as the earliest monuments of Christian literature. They are to be studied as impartially as the literature of any other religion and with no preliminary presuppositions. We must not attempt to superimpose common ideas upon all of the books, nor seek to make them agree with later creeds of the Church. Each book must be examined separately to discover the original author, readers, date, and the circumstances under which it was written. It can only be understood as we lay our own interests and prejudices aside and seek to put ourselves in the position of the author and his first readers. Obviously, some knowledge of the historical background is necessary if such an endeavor is to be successful. No Confucian book is intelligible apart from some knowledge of Chinese life. By an historical approach to the Bible, we would study early Christian literature in the same objective way.

It should be clear that we cannot expect to understand an ancient book like the Bible without the use of "helps." Protestants have traditionally laid emphasis upon the illumination of the Holy Spirit. It is right to stress that a religious message can only be received by a mind which is receptive to religious truth. In that sense, God must interpret his own word. But the Holy Spirit does not provide exact information concerning the ideas of ancient cultures. For these we must turn to the patient labors of the scholars who provide these helps.

Some devout Christians have been fearful to apply historical method to the study of their sacred writings. Consciously or unconsciously, they have taken as the goal of Biblical study the defense of certain inherited conclusions about authorship, date, and the interpretation of Biblical books. It has sometimes been taken for granted, for instance, that it is more religious to ascribe the fourth Gospel to John, the son of Zebedee, than to question that belief. We hold, however, that such an attitude is based on mistaken assumptions. If God is a God of truth, nothing is more religious than the unbiased pursuit of truth. If a fact is a fact, it cannot be irreligious to accept it. The value of Christian truth is not diminished by the discovery that Second Peter is a second-century document, and that Ephesians is not a letter to the city where Paul worked longest in Asia Minor. The Christian's duty is not to defend ancient traditions, but to use all of the advances of modern knowledge to discover the truth about Christian origins.

The study of history is a much-needed discipline for all Christians. We believe in the coming of a better world, and of better men and women to live in that world. From one standpoint we deal continuously in "wishful thinking." Though we believe intensely in the reality of those dreams, we must never lose our touch with present reality. Wishful desires on our part have nothing to do with a discovery of the truth about the writing of the New Testament books. Only by a painstaking survey of the historical evidence can we discover the external facts about the books of the Bible and come to a true interpretation of their contents. Such discipline prepares the way for a knowledge of God. Our wishes do not determine the nature of God. We must obediently listen to the revelation of himself. In studying the books where we believe that revelation is found most fully, we stand in especial need of every safeguard against "wishful thinking." When the sincere Christian becomes fully conscious of these dangers, he will feel the obligation to follow objective, historical method in his study of the Bible.

That leads us to *the religious approach* to the Bible. There are scholars who have only a strictly historical interest in its pages. That is not true of the average member of a Christian Church. Sheer historical curiosity about the origins of our faith will not motivate many to a continuous study of the Bible. If these books do not have some bearing upon questions which are of current, religious significance, there is little hope of promoting a widespread study of the Bible. To recover the ideas of ancient Christians simply for its own sake is not an enterprise in which many can be expected to engage. By a religious approach we mean one which seeks to discover those values which are of significance for today.

This point of view must be clearly distinguished from what we have called "the devotional approach" to the Bible. The latter is carried on quite independently of historical study. The religious approach seeks first of all to discover exactly what the author was trying to say to his readers. But it does not stop there; it goes on to ask a further question: What does this mean to me now? We must not expect ancient books to speak according to our thought forms, nor would we disregard the discoveries which have come in the development of Christian experience. But the Bible stands in a unique place among religious literature if it contains a message which we find of ultimate significance. This approach would seek the religious values as they emerge from historical study.

The following brief chapters are written from the point of view of a union of these last two approaches. The record of Christian origins will be examined in as impartial a spirit as a record of the origins of Buddhism. We do not have conclusions to defend, but facts to discover. Nevertheless, the author seeks constantly to bear in mind that these pages are not written for the benefit of historians, but for men and women who would not study the Bible long if they did not find in it a genuine word of life. After all, this little collection of Greek documents is imperishable because they do speak to the eternal need of men.

QUESTIONS FOR MEDITATION AND DISCUSSION

1. It is sometimes said, "If we cannot believe in *every* word of the Bible, how can we accept any of it as true?" Do we take such a position toward any other piece of writing?

2. How could we use an infallible Bible without infallible interpreters?

3. Is historical information necessary for a devotional use of the Bible?

4. What illustrations of allegorical interpretation of Biblical passages can you give from your own experience?

5. How many of your friends read the Bible for its literary value? Should they? Do you?

6. Do you find modern colloquial translations easier to understand than the King James Version? How often do you use them in your church school?

7. What do you understand by "historical method"?

8. In what way is the value of a Biblical book affected by a decision as to its author and date?

9. Distinguish between a "devotional" and a "religious" approach to the Bible? How important do you find this distinction to be?

10. In what sense do you believe that the Bible is the revealed word of God?

A SMALL REFERENCE SHELF

Modern Translations
  The New English Bible.
  J. B. Phillips, *The New Testament in Modern English.*
  Revised Standard Version.

Introductions to the New Testament
  E. J. Goodspeed, *An Introduction to the New Testament.*
  F. C. Grant, *An Introduction to New Testament Thought.*

Commentary
  The Abingdon Bible Commentary, edited by F. C. Eiselen, Edwin Lewis, and David G. Downey. The best single volume, combining articles about the Bible with a Commentary on Old and New Testament.

Dictionaries of the Bible
  M. S. and J. L. Miller, *Harper's Dictionary of the Bible.*
  The Interpreter's Dictionary of the Bible, 4 volumes.

Books About the Use of the Bible
  Fred Denbeaux, *Understanding the Bible.*
  Robert E. Koenig, *The Use of the Bible with Adults.*
  Charles M. Laymon, *The Message of the Bible.*

Books on How the Bible Was Formed
  William Barclay, *The Making of the Bible.*
  Edward P. Blair, *The Bible and You.*

Present Trends in Bible Study
  Martin Marty, *New Directions in Biblical Thought.*

CHAPTER ONE

THE GOSPEL BEFORE THE GOSPELS

JESUS wrote no books. He was not a scholar in a cloistered study but a man of the people. He did not live in an age when the masses of men could be reached by the printed page. In the beginning was the word and deed of Jesus. Christianity did not arise among a literary group, but among simple people who listened with joy to his words and were drawn by his deeds of kindness.

The clearest picture of the method of Jesus is to be found in his parable of the sower. It is a reflective meditation upon the work of every teacher. As the farmer sows his seed, so the teacher scatters his word. In each case the result depends upon the soil. Among the many hearers of Jesus, twelve were drawn more closely to him. They traveled with him and helped him in his ministry. Doubtless they heard many of his utterances over and over again. The Master was not a preacher addressing the same congregation week after week, but an itinerant missionary who from village to village proclaimed the need for repentance in view of the coming kingdom of God.

All that we know of the teaching of Jesus depends upon the memory of the disciples who heard these words. Enterprising publishers may print red-letter testaments, but it is wise to remember that we do not have a single sentence which Jesus wrote. There is no reason to believe that anything was written down during his lifetime. No newspaper reports of sermons or deeds were ever available. It is ridiculous to think of

Matthew or any other disciple sitting down at night, as a devoted Boswell to his Johnson, writing down the beautiful things which Jesus had said that day. It is possible that Jesus cast some of his teaching into rhythmic form and that it was committed to memory by the disciples. But when it is observed that even the Lord's Prayer did not circulate among the early Christians in an absolutely fixed form, one must be cautious in making any claims of this kind.

The crucifixion came to the disciples as a terrible disillusionment. Apparently, they returned to Galilee to resume their former work. According to the earliest account, Cephas, or Peter, was the first to receive the overpowering conviction that Jesus had been raised from the dead. Soon a group of disciples, estimated at one hundred and twenty, was back again in Jerusalem. They lived together in close fellowship and proclaimed that the Jesus who had been crucified had been declared God's Anointed One by the resurrection from the dead. It should be borne in mind that the Christian Church did not develop in Galilee, where Jesus had carried on his ministry. The apostles apparently did not continue their work primarily among former hearers of Jesus. Outside of the original nucleus, the Church was not composed of those who had been gathered by Jesus' own preaching. The Church was an outgrowth of belief in his resurrection.

The earliest message of the apostles was not that Jesus was a martyred rabbi who had left behind him a noble body of teaching. It was not that there had lived in Galilee an example whom all should follow. Their message was not biographical information about the Jesus whom some had known and loved. It was first of all *good news from God*. His Messiah, or

Anointed One, had appeared in the person of this Jesus who had been crucified. But God had vindicated him by raising him from the dead, of which they were witnesses.

The earliest form of the Christian message which can be reached is given by Paul in a letter to the Church at Corinth written about 54 A. D. He tells us not simply the gospel which he preached, but the message which he himself had received. "I delivered unto you first of all that which also I received: that Christ died for our sins according to the scriptures; and that he was buried; and that he hath been raised on the third day according to the scriptures; and that he appeared to Cephas; then to the twelve. . . ." When one examines the earliest sermons reported in the Acts of the Apostles, he finds complete corroboration. The passion and resurrection were the center of the message.

Naturally, Peter, James, and John expanded this simple word in greater detail. Men wanted to know *how* Christ had died for their sins. The earliest formulation of any part of the story of Jesus was undoubtedly an account of the betrayal, Last Supper, trial, and crucifixion. In fact, scholars are now convinced that this is the only section of the life of Jesus which was ever told with any thought of historical sequence. We must not expect that these enthusiastic preachers told the Passion story as a detached newspaper reporter might have observed it. It was reported as seen through the eyes of faith of the disciples who had come to believe that here was God's decisive invasion of history.

Stranger to us is the emphasis in the earliest Christian message on *the fulfillment of scripture.* But it is quite understandable when we put ourselves in the position of the earliest believers. How could they believe that a criminal who had suffered the death penalty was nevertheless the Anointed of God? It was only conceivable if this was part of the career which God had planned for him. The Old Testament was not read from the historical point of view, but as a series of predictions of events to come. In the Passion story as we read it, we find many references to the fulfillment of prophecy. The accounts of the earliest preaching, as given in the Acts of the Apostles, emphasize that the death of Jesus was not contrary to the will of God, but that it had been anticipated in Scripture. The cross did not mean defeat, but had been God's purpose from the beginning.

The Bible of the earliest Christians was the Old Testament. It was the sacred Word of God. But most of the early Christians were too poor to have copies for themselves. It would not have been practicable for itinerant missionaries to carry with them all of these bulky scrolls. Hence the necessity arose for collections of proof-texts, series of passages which were valuable in argument with the Jews. When the same Old Testament passage is cited by several New Testament writers, the probability arises that it was prominent in such a collection. The evangelist Matthew seems to be quoting from such a compilation when he introduces a series of passages with such phrases as "that it might be fulfilled which was spoken through the prophet." When Paul gives a whole series of passages upon a point, it is probable that he was not collecting them for the first time. *Telling the story of Jesus involved showing that he was the fulfillment of God's long purpose in history.*

Who was this Jesus who had died for their sins? He

was "a man approved of God unto you by mighty works and wonders and signs which God did by him in the midst of you"; he was one "who went about doing good, and healing all that were oppressed of the devil; for God was with him." But surely the actual sermons of Peter contained many illustrations of these claims. Every evangelist needed a fund of anecdotes in order to describe this activity more vividly. The details of time and place of such incidents were not important. There was no aim to give what we would call a "life of Jesus." Peter and the others would simply describe these things in order to support the faith in Jesus to which men were invited.

Various classifications have been proposed for the isolated gospel incidents. We may distinguish here three important types or "forms." The first are sometimes called *pronouncement stories*. In these the emphasis is not upon the incident itself, but a word of Jesus is the focus of interest. Typical of these is the defense of the Sabbath violation by the disciples with the word, "The sabbath was made for man, and not man for the sabbath." There is no indication as to where the field was from which the disciples had plucked the grain. The only important fact was that the event took place on a Sabbath. It was told in order to illustrate the conviction to which believers should come, "that the Son of man is lord even of the sabbath."

A second group is composed of *tales* illustrating the *wonder-working power of Jesus*. In a world where various healing gods, one, for example, such as Aesculapius, were proclaimed, the Christian preachers announced a greater Saviour than any of these. The healing of a leper and of a violent demoniac illus-

trated the power of Jesus over disease. Other stories
were circulated claiming his power over nature. To
those who read how Elisha had fed one hundred men
with twenty barley loaves, it was related how Jesus had
fed five thousand with five loaves and a few fish.

We might designate the third group as *epiphany
stories*. They were told in order to bring out the
divine character of the mission of Jesus. The story
of the baptism of Jesus is an example. Our first
thought in reading that account is of the problem
which every young man faces in the choice of his
vocation. That was certainly not the standpoint, however, from which the evangelists told the story. They
were not interested in how Jesus solved his life problem. They wanted to affirm the belief that the divine
choice had rested upon Jesus. Fulfillment had come
to the word of the psalm,

> "Thou art my son,
> This day have I begotten thee."

We must remember, then, that the stories about
Jesus were circulated by word of mouth in the interest of the preaching mission. They were not simply
anecdotes from an eventful life, nor did anyone think
in terms of a biography of Jesus. They were re-
counted in order to awaken faith in him as God's
Anointed. He would soon come in glory. All men
must repent and be ready for his coming.

A call to repentance implies some norm of conduct.
Particularly when former Gentiles were brought into
the church there was need for an ethical catechism
which would set forth the moral standards for believers in Jesus. To join the cult of Isis or Attis might
not call for any essential change in conduct; but if

anyone was to become a follower of the Lord Jesus Christ, he must become a "new creature."   Already in the letters of Paul, the earliest Christian documents which we possess, there is evidence of a collection of the words of Jesus.   Whether that was written, or as yet oral, we have no means of knowing.   Even though Paul laid so much stress upon the heavenly, exalted Christ, the words of the historical Jesus were for him a final authority.   Where such words were known, the issue was settled.   Where none were at hand, as in the case of the union of a believer and a nonbeliever, he offered his own best judgment, which he held was under the influence of the living Christ.

The nature of such a collection of the words of Jesus may be inferred from a papyrus fragment from Oxyrhynchus in Egypt.   It consists of a series of miscellaneous words, each introduced by "Jesus says."   While this particular collection is late and does not add much that is authentic to what we know from our canonical Gospels, it shows the detached and isolated form in which the words of Jesus were originally collected and preserved.   No long sermons were recalled. In the main, only separate sayings were preserved, quite independent of context.   These pithy maxims, poetic strophes, and prophetic proclamations were brought together according to more or less arbitrary schemes to aid the memory.

One of the most assured results of the modern study of the Gospels is that one of the sources used in our Gospels of Luke and Matthew was a document or documents which consisted mainly of such a collection of words.   The symbol "Q" is used to refer to it, the first letter of the German word "Quelle," meaning "source."   Wide difference of opinion exists concerning the conjecture; it should be remembered that no copies have survived; but there is no other hypothesis which offers so satisfactory an explanation of the common material in these Gospels. Doubtless several such collections arose to meet the needs of the various churches. Divergences naturally arose in the report of some of the words of Jesus. In one community a word might be applied in one direction; in another church it would be given a different application. Likewise, a process of translation was inevitably involved in making words of Jesus available for the churches. Jesus had spoken in Aramaic, but quite early a majority of the Christians spoke Greek and needed a collection in that language. There are a few difficult passages in our Gospels where it is conjectured that there was mistranslation of the original Aramaic.

We all know from experience that stories are remembered long after everything else which a speaker has said has faded from our memory. Though the parable was a current form used by religious teachers, it is easy to see what a master Jesus was by comparing those reported from him with those ascribed to others. Good stories are sometimes remembered when the original context is forgotten. Occasionally this caused difficulty for the later evangelists. They were eager to use what was reported from Jesus, but in some cases were puzzled as to the original application. On the whole, however, the parables are among the most distinctive and authentic of the teaching reported from Jesus.

The gospel existed long before the Gospels for it is not a book but a message. For at least thirty-five years after the death of Jesus there was no written Gospel.

The living word was borne by fervent messengers. The life preceded the record. The Church came before the book. Its message was the good news of God's redeeming act for men in Jesus Christ.

BOOKS FOR FURTHER STUDY

Gunther Bornkamm, *Jesus of Nazareth*.
Charles M. Laymon, *The Life and Teachings of Jesus*.
Vincent Taylor, *Formation of the Gospel Tradition*.

SUGGESTIONS FOR BIBLE STUDY

1. Read the sermon summaries in Acts 2. 14-39 and 10. 34-43 noting the time it would take to deliver each. How much longer would the actual sermons have been? What do we learn of the content of the earliest preaching? How would Peter have elaborated his message?

2. Read the passion story in one of the Gospels noting the emphasis on fulfillment of scripture. Consult the following passages in Matthew: 1. 23; 2. 6; 2. 15; 2. 17-18; 4. 14-16; 8. 17; 12. 17-21; 13. 35; 21. 4-5; 27. 9.

3. Read Acts 7. 1-53. What does this show concerning interest in the Old Testament?

4. Compare carefully the following passages: Mark 8. 12; Matthew 16. 4; 12. 40; Luke 11. 30. Do you think that Jesus said all of these? How did such different formulations of the words of Jesus arise in the community?

5. Contrast Matthew 5. 1-13 and Luke 6. 20-23. Are they two versions of the same series of words?

6. Read the following additional illustrations of the three different types of incidents described in the text: Mark 2. 1-12; 5. 21-43; 9. 2-8.

7. Read carefully Luke 16. 1-13. Do you believe that the evangelist has correctly understood the story of Jesus? Does it really teach the value of almsgiving?

8. Some people today are primarily interested in the religious experiences of the man Jesus. What bearing does the interest of the first-century Christians have on our ability to reach the experiences of Jesus? Of what sig-

nificance is it that Jesus was from the outset an object of faith for the community?

9. What experiences in your own life are most analogous to those of the disciples, when they sought to recall words and deeds of Jesus after his death and resurrection, although before that time they had kept no records?

CHAPTER TWO

THE MOST IMPORTANT GOSPEL—MARK

ABOUT the year 70 A. D. the most important book of Christendom was written. Its author was not a man of literary attainments, but he had the greatest theme of all time. His opening words were "The beginning of the gospel of Jesus Christ." Our use of the word gospel to designate a book is due to him. All later attempts to tell the story took his work as a starting-point.

According to the earliest tradition of the Church, the author of this little book was John Mark. If that is the case, he was exceptionally well equipped to undertake the task of weaving into a connected account the stories which a generation of Christian preachers had used. He had been associated with Paul in his earlier work, and is cordially mentioned in one of the apostle's latest letters. According to extra-Biblical tradition, Mark had served as interpreter for Peter; he is affectionately mentioned in the Epistle bearing his name. More than that, Mark was a kinsman of Barnabas and had come out of the earliest Jerusalem community. His mother's home had been a meeting place of that group. It is an attractive conjecture that Mark himself was the young lad mentioned in 14. 51 who lost his only garment in a hasty flight at the capture of Jesus. In that case, the room of the Last Supper might have been the home of his parents.

Too much importance, however, should not be assigned to these guesses. There are passages in the

Gospel which are exceedingly difficult to assign to one with his background. In any case, Mark was not an eyewitness of the ministry of Jesus. We are not to think of the story that he tells as particularly that of Peter. He gives us the Gospel as it had been proclaimed by many missionaries.

The earliest tradition located the writing of the Gospel at Rome after the martyrdom of Peter about 64 A. D. It would appear that the first generation was passing away. Simon of Cyrene, who bore the cross for Jesus, is referred to as the father of Alexander and Rufus. Since Paul sent greetings to a Rufus in Romans 16. 13, we cannot help wondering if this was the son of the crossbearer. In that case he would be known personally to the first readers of this Gospel. We know from Paul's letter that the Church at Rome was predominately Gentile. It is clear that Mark wrote for non-Jews, for he took time to explain their peculiar customs. Yet he was close to the Palestinian background of his story, inserting no less than eight phrases in the original Aramaic language. He wrote in a vivid, narrative style, but it is colloquial and unliterary in character.

We do Mark a very great injustice if we think of him setting about the task of writing a life of Jesus. The materials were not at hand, and that was not his aim. There was no attempt to trace character development, nor to delineate the inner life of Jesus. The theme was *the gospel,* the good news of what God had done for men in and through his Son, Jesus. The arrangement of material was not chronological but topical. A consecutive narrative of events was not important for belief in the gospel message. It follows that it is not possible for us to write a consecutive life

of Jesus today for the simple reason that none of our
sources offers us the basis for it.

The main outline of events was given by the traditional preaching. The good news began with the
work of John, the Baptist. There followed the
Messianic designation of Jesus at his baptism, and the
victory over Satan in the wilderness. The author included only a very few sections of teaching to the disciples. That was not a careless omission, for Mark
aimed to give the *preaching* rather than the teaching
of the Church. The first half of the Gospel, recording Galilean incidents, comes to a climax in the
Messianic confession by Peter. From then to the end,
the gospel of the saving death of Jesus is set forth. It
is lighted in advance by the transfiguration scene and
leads inexorably to the empty tomb. Our earliest
manuscripts end abruptly with 16. 8, where the women
flee from the tomb; "for trembling and astonishment
had come upon them: and they said nothing to any
one; for they were afraid." Our English Bibles usually
print the longer of the conclusions, added in the second
century. We have no means of knowing how Mark
originally completed his work.

In a sense, all of our evangelists were compilers and
arrangers of the common tradition used by the early
missionaries. They were not so much authors as
editors. Even Mark probably incorporated some written materials into his Gospel; this applies with greatest probability to the collection of controversies in
2. 1 to 3. 6, the group of parables in 4. 1-34, and the
apocalyptic discourse embodied in 13. 5-27. Yet we
should do full justice to the individuality which the
evangelists show in their arrangement and emphases.
We shall take up in order four of the interests which

Mark reveals. The material was given to him by the tradition, but he put his own peculiar stamp upon it.

Jesus is presented as *the Son of God with power*. From the outset Mark makes it plain that he is not recording the life of an ordinary human being. The ministry is opened by a typical Sabbath in Capernaum marked by a series of healing incidents. A cycle of three great deeds—the exorcism of the Gadarene demoniac, the healing of the woman with the issue of blood, and the raising of Jairus's daughter—reveals the power of faith in the Son of God in contrast to the lack of faith in his home town. The One who multiplied the loaves and fishes and stilled the waves was not One whom the disciples were expected to imitate. Jesus was not presented by Mark as an example whom men could be expected to copy, but as their Saviour.

It is true that there are indications of the very real humanity of Jesus which later evangelists dropped because these were offensive to their faith. Matthew was troubled that Jesus should present himself for a baptism described as for the forgiveness of sins and introduced a conversation designed to explain it (Matthew 3. 15). Since it seemed to him inappropriate to call Jesus the carpenter, he changed it to the carpenter's son (Matthew 13. 55). He did not think that Jesus could have refused to be called "good," so he changed the Markan text to read, "Why askest thou me concerning that which is good?" (Matthew 19. 17.) Nevertheless, the aim of Mark was to show the unique power of Jesus, the Son of God, which set him apart from all other men. Whatever our own beliefs about Jesus may be, those of Mark cannot be mistaken.

The Christ of Mark was pre-eminently *a Christ of controversy*. We sometimes forget that the phrase, "the Prince of Peace" is drawn from prophecies of the Old Testament. It certainly does not fit the Jesus of Mark, who is represented in continual struggle with successive opponents. Typical controversies deal with the power of Jesus to forgive sins, his eating with sinners, the observance of the Sabbath, the source of Jesus' power, the validity of the traditions of the elders, the permissibility of divorce, the authority of Jesus, civil obedience, and the resurrection.

Why should these be so prominent in Mark's story? For one reason, they tended to show how Jesus had been rejected by the Jewish leaders. But that was not the most important reason, for in the eyes of all early Christians the crucifixion was ultimately the will of God for their redemption. Much more important was the fact that many of the controversies recorded by Mark concerned issues with which his readers were then dealing. Some modern religious educators have approached the Bible from the standpoint of finding solutions for our modern problems. It is worth remembering that men like Mark wrote for the purpose of helping to solve the problems of the first Christians.

Not only were many of the controversies *selected* according to the needs of the Roman readers. In his narrative Mark did not hesitate to *adapt* the account to the interests of the new audience. In Palestine women could not divorce their husbands, but Roman women suffered no such disability. Hence Mark extended the original word of Jesus to cover the new situation. To Jesus' word that the only real defilement was from within, he added the interpretation "making all meats clean." His Gentile readers were more interested in that than in ceremonial handwashing. It is clear from Acts 10. 9ff. and Galatians 2. 11ff. that Peter did not draw this conclusion until some years after the death of Jesus. But Mark was thinking much less of what disciples had actually heard in a house in Palestine forty years earlier than what the attitude of Jesus had come to mean for his followers through the perspective of years.

Mark assumed that *the Messiahship of Jesus had been a secret.* The question might well be asked, "If Jesus performed all of the mighty works which are recorded in this book, why did not the Jews themselves believe on him?" At the time when he wrote, it was already apparent that the Christian testimony would be accepted by only a small body of Jews. Paul had wrestled with this difficult problem in the Epistle to the Romans and had suggested that the hearts of the Jews had been purposely hardened by God. Mark also has the theory that Jesus spoke in parables in order that the masses might not understand. The mystery of the Kingdom was given only unto a few. The rest were hardened, according to the words of Isaiah, lest they might turn and repent.

Mark presents a Jesus who publicly proclaimed the coming kingdom of God, but never spoke openly of his own Messiahship. Only the demons recognized who their Master was. After healings, Jesus is represented as commanding silence. First near Caesarea Philippi was the person of Jesus a matter of discussion with the disciples. When Peter affirmed on their behalf that Jesus was the Christ, he was met with the charge to tell no man. Nowhere does Jesus affirm his Messiahship until the hearing before the high priest.

It is clear that Jesus was put to death on a Messianic charge, but modern interpreters are not in agreement as to the truth behind Mark's theory of the Messianic secret. We shall not discuss the possible alternatives here, since our purpose is not to reconstruct the career of Jesus but to understand the story which each succeeding evangelist sought to tell. Mark represents the Messiahship of Jesus as a carefully guarded secret during the lifetime of the Master.

Writing for a Church which had just passed through the persecution under Nero, Mark composed *a gospel exalting martyrdom*. The central theme was the martyr death of Jesus. This stood apart from all others as "the ransom for many." The shadow of the cross falls as early as the second chapter, where the taking away of the bridegroom is envisaged. Mark makes it clear that death did not come upon Jesus unexpectedly. Three times the details of the Passion are explicitly predicted. It was not a fate which he was called upon to endure, but the very goal of his career; and every prediction of the Passion is made to culminate in the expectation of God's vindication in the resurrection.

Such a martyr called for followers who would be willing to take up their cross. James and John are told that the road to the chief seats in the new age did not lie alone through the sacraments of the Church, but the cup and baptism of martyrdom. Men and women who had seen friends and loved ones thrown to the wild beasts in the arena were the first readers of these words, "Whosoever would save his life shall lose it; and whosoever shall lose his life for my sake and the gospel's shall save it. . . . For whosoever shall be ashamed of me and of my words in this adulterous and sinful generation, the Son of man also shall be ashamed of him, when he cometh in the glory of his Father with the holy angels." "Before governors and kings shall ye stand for my sake, for a testimony unto them. . . . And when they . . . deliver you up, be not anxious beforehand what ye shall speak: but whatever shall be given you in that hour, that speak ye. . . . And ye shall be hated of all men for my name's sake: but he that endureth to the end, the same shall be saved." These were not vague predictions to the first readers. They expressed the grim reality through which they had passed.

It is clear that Mark offers us very much more than the simple matter-of-fact story of a reporter. He gives us throughout a Christian interpretation of the facts. In a very real sense he has written a book of theology. Confronting the needs of the Church of his time, when the first generation of leaders was passing away, he set forth the good news of Jesus Christ. It is a book of faith, not of history. That does not mean that what he recorded was not true. It means that the facts of that life are seen through eyes illumined by a generation of Christian experience.

What does Mark have to offer those of us who live in such a different time? It is the same good news of God. Naturally, we shall state it in a different framework of experience. Nineteen centuries have contributed to our understanding of that Gospel. We shall make new applications for our age, as Mark did for his. But the essential Christian message is an interpretation of the life of Jesus in terms of an ultimate word of God for men. That is Mark's theme, and that is his message to the twentieth century as well as to the first.

BOOKS FOR FURTHER STUDY

B. H. Branscomb, *The Gospel of Mark*. (Commentary on the Moffatt translation.)

Sherman Johnson, *The Gospel According to St. Mark*.

Paul S. Minear, *The Gospel According to Mark* (Layman's Bible Commentary, vol. 17).

SUGGESTIONS FOR THE STUDY OF MARK

1. If possible, procure a synopsis of the Gospels so that the dependence of Matthew and Luke upon Mark may be observed. The best are E. D. Burton and E. J. Goodspeed, *A Harmony of the Synoptic Gospels*, and W. E. Bundy, *A Syllabus and Synopsis of the First Three Gospels*.

2. Note the following passages illustrating characteristics of Mark mentioned in the text: 7. 3-4; 5. 41; 7. 34.

3. Study carefully the following controversies: 2. 1 to 3. 6; 3. 22-30; 7. 1-23; 10. 2-10; 11. 23-33; 12. 13-27. Consider what special interest Roman Christians might have had in such issues as civil obedience and Sabbath observance. To what extent do the words of Jesus on these subjects afford solutions to our problems?

4. Read the cycle of great deeds in 5. 1 to 6. 6. Note the fuller narrative style delighting in details.

5. Study the following passages in order to see how Jesus is represented as being recognized by the demons, not by the men who were possessed by them: 1. 24; 1. 34; 3. 11.

6. How does Mark's interest in Jesus differ from your own? How would you explain his theory of the Messianic secret?

7. What are the chief inadequacies which you find in Mark's Gospel? Why is it not more popular with average Bible readers?

CHAPTER THREE

THE MOST INFLUENTIAL GOSPEL MATTHEW

WHEN any modern Christian is asked to quote a saying of Jesus which is found in more than one Gospel, it is almost certain that he will follow the wording of the Gospel according to Matthew. We repeat his form of the Lord's Prayer in church and memorize his version of the Beatitudes in church school. So well did this Christian rabbi perform his task of presenting an ethical catechism, that it came to occupy the first place, not only in the order of Gospels, but in influence upon the Church.

From the second century, it has been assumed that its author was the publican by the name of Matthew, which replaces the name of Levi which had stood in Mark. Modern scholars are agreed, however, that this is impossible. The book is clearly dependent upon our Gospel of Mark, which is certainly not from an eyewitness. The Gospel according to Matthew is best described as a revised and enlarged edition of Mark, incorporating as it does the substance of six hundred and five of its six hundred and sixty-six verses. It is incredible that one of the original twelve disciples should have been dependent in this way upon one who had never walked with Jesus in Galilee. It may be that Matthew's name came to be associated with the Gospel because he had compiled one of the sources utilized by our evangelist. Some think that this was the "Sayings" source, usually designated "Q." Others conjecture that it was a collection of Old Testament proof-texts.

If the actual evangelist must remain anonymous for us, he is by no means unknown. We are better acquainted with him than with the actual Matthew. He was a former Jew who believed firmly in the world-wide mission of Christianity. He opens his book with the missionary story of the coming of the Gentile Wise Men to worship the "king of the Jews," and ends with the command, "Go ye into all the world and preach the gospel to the whole creation." It is probably one of his sources which rejects even a mission to the Samaritans. Nevertheless, he does not think of Jesus as the end of the law, as did Paul, but as the giver of a new law. The evangelist wrote at a time when the perils of a law-free gospel were apparent. The Church which had accepted men on the basis of faith only had become anything but the pure virgin which Paul had envisaged. There were now many members who were like tares among the wheat. The Church had gathered all kinds of men and women into its net, both good and bad. Some were no longer faithful and diligent in good works. They were by no means ready for the coming of their Lord. In such a situation, this evangelist calls for *righteousness;* his is the only Gospel where this word appears as a duty of a disciple. By his stress upon the coming of Christ and the nearness of the Judgment, he endeavors to whip up enthusiasm again and improve the ethical discipline of the community. The fire of Gehenna and "weeping and gnashing of teeth" are much more prominent here than in any other Gospel.

We have no certain knowledge concerning its date and locale. The best guess is that it was written in

Syria toward the close of the first Christian century.
Many have located its original home in Antioch, the
great capital city of Syria. Certainly, this would have
been an influential point for its dissemination and the
growth of its influence. Antioch was the second birth-
place of the Church, where the gospel had first been
systematically preached to Greeks, and where the name
"Christian" had first been used to designate the believers. Paul had worked there during his early ministry and Peter had been associated with the Church
according to Galatians 2. 11. It is to be noted that the
legends about Peter are to be found in Matthew rather
than in Mark. He alone tells of the attempt of the
apostle to walk on the water and the promise that he
would be the rock on which the Church should be
built.

The arrangement of material is clearly according to
a fixed plan. The story of the birth of Jesus stands in
chapters 1-2, taken from sources which Matthew alone
used. The account assumes that Joseph and Mary
had lived in Bethlehem and only came to Nazareth
after the flight into Egypt. The Passion and Resurrection story in chapters 26-28 is based on Mark, with
the addition of a few later developments such as the
story of the death of Judas, the dream of Pilate's wife,
and the guard at the tomb. These sections form the
introduction and conclusion to the Gospel.

The material which lies between, in chapters 3-25,
falls naturally into five divisions. The Jewish Law,
or Torah, was composed of five books, our Pentateuch.
Since the evangelist (to whom we shall refer for convenience as Matthew) conceived of Christianity as the
new and higher law, it was fitting that he should write
his Gospel in five books. Each of these is divided into

a narrative section and a teaching section. Each teaching section ends with a similar phrase marking the
transitions—"when Jesus had finished these words."
In order to construct these blocks of material, Matthew rearranged his documents according to a fairly
consistent topical outline. He knew Mark well
enough to select his material freely. We may assume
that he used his other documentary sources in a similar way. Except for the "sayings source," nothing can
be said about these with any certainty. It is to be
recognized, however, that the long speeches assigned
to Jesus are compilations which the evangelist has
made in pursuance of his pedagogical purpose.

The first division may be called the book of *dis-
cipleship*. The narrative section found in chapters
3-4 records the baptism and temptation of Jesus, his
own calling to the divine task. Then follows the calling of the first disciples in Galilee. This affords a
fitting place for the compilation of the ethical teaching of Jesus, setting forth the righteousness which
should exceed the righteousness of the scribes and
Pharisees (chapters 5-7). Moses had ascended a mountain in order to receive from God the tables of stone.
Jesus is represented as ascending a mountain in order
to deliver the fulfillment of that Law, the narrow way
which leads to life. In these chapters there is brought
together a priceless collection of words illustrating the
inward and absolute moral ideals of the Master.

The book of *apostleship* is introduced by a narrative section in which the evangelist collects a series of
great deeds of Jesus (chapters 8-9). While most of
them are taken from Mark, they do not stand here in
the same order. Matthew had no more idea of the
actual order of events than Mark, but he does im-

prove on the topical connection. Illustrations are brought together of the cleansing of a leper, giving sight to the blind, and hearing to the deaf, and the raising of the dead in order to prepare the way for the answer to John, the Baptist, in 11. 2-6. The Messianic expectations of Isaiah had been fulfilled in the ministry of Jesus.

The teaching for this book (9. 37 to 11. 1 deals with the instructions to the apostles as they carry on the ministry of Jesus. To the words of commission as they stood in Mark and also in "Q" he joined other appropriate sayings concerning their mission in Palestine. Naturally, the wording of some of these reflects the experiences of the apostles after the death of Jesus. Here as elsewhere we must remember the conviction of the early church that Jesus was not an absent Lord. "Where two or three are gathered together in my name, there am I in the midst of them." Memory and reflection were united as they sought to serve their risen Lord.

The third book cannot be characterized so simply. We see misunderstanding and offense and the gathering opposition. John, the Baptist, hesitates and the Galilean cities reject the Master. The Pharisees oppose at every hand, and even the family of Jesus do not believe. The divine revelation was hid from the wise and understanding and revealed only unto babes. Possibly the best description of the book is that of *the hidden and revealed mystery*. Throughout the narrative section, which extends from 11. 2 to 12. 50, the mighty failed to read the signs of the times though in their midst was "more than" either Jonah or Solomon.

As the teaching section for this book, Matthew used

the parable chapter drawn from Mark, expanded by other parables of a like nature (13. 1-53). You will find the key to the chapter in the conception that the mystery of the kingdom of God is given only to the disciples. Though others oppose and reject, a small beginning has been made with this little group, from which in the Divine Providence the kingdom of God will ultimately come. "Blessed are your eyes, for they see; and your ears, for they hear."

From this point on, Matthew follows the order of Mark without change. We can no longer inquire, therefore, why he arranged his material as he did. The narrative section of the fourth book, extending from 14. 1 to 17. 27, deals largely with apparently aimless wandering outside of Galilee. The climax is the confession of Peter at Caesarea Philippi. Belief in the Messiahship of Jesus was fundamental to the Christian Church. Matthew weakens the impression made by Jesus' command for silence by inserting into the Markan story the affirmation that this was revealed by God, and that Peter was the rock upon which the Church should be built. It is probable that this was Antiochian tradition claiming the supremacy for Peter as opposed to James, the brother of Jesus, who was the leader at Jerusalem.

It is fitting that the speech for this fourth section should be a series of *instructions for the church* (18. 1-35). Treatment of the humble and weak members, discipline of the erring, and forgiveness for those who wrong us are the chief themes. It is interesting to note that in Paul's treatment of the case of incest in 1 Corinthians 5, he follows the procedure outlined in this chapter. It should be observed that the powers of binding and loosing which are assigned to Peter alone in 16. 19 are given to all of the apostles in 18. 18. The words were current Jewish designations for forbidding (binding) and permitting (loosing).

The journey to Jerusalem and the events in the Holy City are described in the narrative section of book V (chapters 19-23). Notice that Mark is followed throughout with some additions. These include the parable of the laborers in the vineyard, with its strong repudiation of the idea of merit which was characteristic of much Jewish teaching, and also a long tirade against the Pharisees in chapter 23. While there is little doubt that Jesus spoke sharp words of attack upon the Pharisees, most of us will be glad to assign some of the venom of this chapter to the Jewish Christians who had suffered so severely at the hands of the leaders of the synagogues.

As Jesus approached his end, it was fitting that the teaching for this last book should deal with *the future*. Following his customary procedure, Matthew combined the apocalyptic speech in Mark 13 and the apocalypse which had stood in "Q" into one address extending over chapters 24-25. We should remember that the elaborate descriptions of the signs of the end were characteristic of Jewish literature of the time. We are not to think of this material as giving an infallible timetable of the ages, but as part of the Jewish inheritance of the Church. It has already been noted that Matthew lived at a time when the primitive expectation of the imminent coming of Jesus was beginning to wane, and the Church to grow lax. Matthew sought to reawaken that expectation Though Christ was like a Lord who had gone into a distant country, he would nevertheless return and reckon with his servants; though he was like a bridegroom delayed in his coming, he would yet arrive. But would the Church be ready? In the Judgment Day it would not suffice to say, "Lord, Lord." Only those who do the will of God by their acts of kindness to the brethren of the Son of man would enter into the joy of their Lord.

It is apparent from this survey of the contents of the first Gospel that the evangelist thought of Jesus primarily as Messiah and teacher. Of these two, the modern Church is inclined to stress the latter. It is Jesus the teacher of a noble way of life which has appealed most strongly to our generation. The Messianic idea does not have the same contact with our experience. We should remember, however, that this belief primarily affirmed that the Jesus who taught the ideals of the Sermon on the Mount was also indissolubly linked with the Judge of the universe. These were not simply the beautiful dreams of a Galilean peasant, but the eternal will of God.

Matthew does not neglect to stress the forgiving grace of God. Though the garment of righteousness cannot be neglected, the invitation to the banquet of God is irrespective of merit. It is the will of God to *give* unto all alike, as shown in the parable of the workers in the vineyard. The Gospel of Matthew shows clearly that Jesus was not simply an ethical teacher. Here we see one whose central interest was *religious*. The way to life is proclaimed against a background of divine grace and judgment. Jesus is the authoritative teacher because he sets forth the will of God.

BOOKS FOR FURTHER STUDY

Edward P. Blair, *Jesus in the Gospel of Matthew.*

B. Harvie Branscomb and Ernest W. Saunders, *The Message of Jesus.*

Floyd V. Filson, *The Gospel According to St. Matthew.*

F. C. Grant, *The Gospels: Their Origin and Their Growth.*

SUGGESTIONS FOR THE STUDY OF MATTHEW

1. Observe the emphasis on righteousness in 5. 20 and 6. 33; read the parables which recognize a division within the Church: 13. 24-30, 36-43, 47-50.

2. Observe the importance of Antioch in Acts 11. 21; 15. 3, and Galatians 2. 11ff.

3. Read the special stories about Peter found only in Matthew: 14. 28-31; 16. 17-19; 17. 24-27.

4. Note the formula concluding each of the five books: 7. 28; 11. 1; 13. 53; 19. 1; 26. 1. If possible, use a harmony of the Gospels to read through the five great speeches. Note how the parallels in Luke are to be found scattered over different chapters. Note also how Matthew weaves together similar words into one long speech, while Luke consistently follows one source at a time. Compare especially Matthew 10 with Luke 9. 1-5 and Luke 10. 1-12.

5. Read side by side Matthew 14-15 and Mark 6. 14 to 8. 10, making note of the types of changes made by Matthew. Are most of them editorial, or do you think that they reveal new information from other sources?

6. Is it misleading when Matthew presents Jesus as a new lawgiver? Can the teaching of Jesus be made into a law? Has the Church ever made that mistake?

CHAPTER FOUR

THE MOST POPULAR GOSPEL—JOHN

IN any company of Christian people an informal vote will show that the fourth Gospel is the most popular of all. The devout Christian turns first to its pages for inspiration; it is the first book of the Bible to be translated into a new language. The reflective historian is not at all surprised, for this little book contains the climactic interpretation of the gospel within the New Testament. It speaks directly to the experience of men today because in it the message is taken out of the more specifically Jewish idiom in which the gospel was first proclaimed and translated into the more universal thought-forms of the Hellenistic world.

At the end of the second century the *author* was generally believed to be John, the son of Zebedee. A large majority of modern scholars no longer accept that ascription, though many still believe that his witness is an important element in the story. The Gospel itself makes no claim concerning its authorship. Chapter 21 is an appendix, and we cannot be certain that it is by the same hand. The last verses of this chapter affirm that the author as well as the witness was "the beloved disciple." This is an enigmatical figure who appears only in Jerusalem, and strangely, almost always in competition with Peter. Up until chapter 21 the beloved disciple has always stood first. Here, Peter is given the primacy in feeding the sheep. Some modern scholars have gone so far as to claim that the beloved disciple could not have

49

been a Galilean fisherman, such as John, the son of Zebedee. It must have been a Jerusalem disciple who knew the servants of the high priest and could take the mother of Jesus into his home on the very day of the crucifixion. Others have insisted that this disciple was John and was the unnamed companion of Andrew in 1. 40. Whatever theory we adopt for the identity of the beloved disciple, it would seem to me impossible to hold that he was the author of the Gospel. A man who was too modest to mention his own name, but who referred to himself as "the disciple whom Jesus loved" would be a most unusual character.

The decision concerning authorship must be based not on later apologetic tradition but upon the character and contents of the Gospel itself. We shall find that it is far removed from the primitive Church and its problems and is a statement of the developed faith of the Church at the close of the first century. The author was *a devotional mystic* with both Hebrew and Graeco-Oriental backgrounds. He was an eyewitness not of outward events but of the glory of the only-begotten Son. Despite the word "logos" in the prologue, it is a mistake to see in the book a philosophical document. The author is not indulging in philosophical speculation but is transmitting religious revelation. Christianity is not a higher righteousness, as with Matthew, but the revelation of "the truth" as brought to men by the divine messenger. The author writes in a simple uninvolved style, developing his themes in figures drawn from the most general human experiences. A wedding, birth, water, sickness, and food are used to symbolize the various aspects of the message and at the same time make contact with the universal man of all times and places.

It is generally believed that the fourth evangelist knew both Mark and Luke. In many ways he continues tendencies begun in Luke. But he also had *an independent tradition upon which he meditated* and which is given the precedence at many places over the Synoptic tradition. Modern scholars have come to realize that at many points he adds to our historical information. John (we shall so designate the evangelist for convenience) may well be correct that before the opening of his Galilean ministry Jesus had an earlier ministry in Judea by the side of John, the Baptist. Also, a ministry of some months in Jerusalem near the close of his life is highly probable. It is likely that John is correct in dating the death of Jesus before the Passover instead of on the first day of the feast, as in Mark. Furthermore, we have no reason to doubt that new words of Jesus from genuine tradition were incorporated into the speeches of the fourth Gospel. However, we have no means of identifying them as we do those which have a parallel in the other Gospels.

As they stand, *the speeches* are unquestionably the product of the reflection of the evangelist. A comparison with the Epistle of John shows that the same phrases are used in one place as the author's own and in another as from Jesus. The aim of John was not to reproduce the very words of Jesus. It was to set forth the gospel as he had come to understand it after two or three generations of Christian experience. The speeches in John contain so large an interpretative element that they cannot be used for a reconstruction of the teaching of the historical Jesus. Though they are deeply influenced by the spirit of Jesus, they must be treated as "Johannine theology."

The clue to the understanding of the Gospel is found when we see that the author has read back into the life of Jesus *the contemporary faith of the Church.* His aim is less to reproduce historic fact than to proclaim the truth of the gospel as he has come to know it. The whole career of Jesus is set forth as a revelation of the divine glory. In Mark this was confined to the story of the transfiguration; in John, the whole ministry is a manifestation of the divine radiance. John, the Baptist, announces Jesus in words summing up all of Christian redemptive theology, "Behold, the Lamb of God, that taketh away the sin of the world!" The disciples believe on him as Messiah from the beginning. A Samaritan woman is able to call Jesus by the most universal title in the whole New Testament, Saviour of the world. Jesus is the great "I AM," the epiphany of God. He is made to affirm that "before Abraham was, I am;" he was at one with God in action, knowledge, and being.

In the earlier Gospels, *the controversies* revolved about the interpretation of the law and Jesus' actions in violation of the "traditions of the elders." Here the controversies are even more bitter, but they involve entirely different subjects. The debate is over the authority, the origin, and the power of Jesus himself. His person is the center of dispute, such as it came to be when Church and synagogue stood opposed to each other. We are far removed from a Jesus yearning over the city of Jerusalem. Here he stands in defiant opposition to the "unbelieving Jews." They are sons of the devil rather than Abraham's children.

John presents *a radical reinterpretation of the expectations for the end,* or the eschatological hope. The spirit of truth has guided him into new truth fully as much as it has brought to mind the things which Jesus had actually said in the flesh. *Judgment* is no longer presented as a great assize at the end of the age. It is a present spiritual event which separates men now. We are judged as we choose darkness rather than light and fail to accept the messenger of truth.

Eternal life is no longer thought of in terms of life in the age to come. It is not something which follows the resurrection, but it begins here and now as we believe in Christ. A future resurrection evaporates before the conviction of the gift of a present eternal life which death cannot destroy. Our belief in immortality in contrast to a resurrection on the last day arises from the Gospel of John, and from that alone in the New Testament.

In like manner, *the coming of Christ* is reinterpreted in terms of the new perspective. No longer is it anticipated as an outward coming on the clouds of heaven to inaugurate the judgment. The coming of Christ is presented in John as a spiritual manifestation to the hearts of those who love him and keep his word. It is not an event of the future but of the eternal present. John believed in a Christ who had already come in "a little while" to make his abode with those who had believed in him.

It is no accident that the Gospel of John has contributed so much to the Passion Play at Oberammergau. It is *a series of dramatic incidents*. Chapter one may well be read as a series of tableaux. Such an interview as that with the woman at the well in Samaria reveals the skill of the dramatist. The conversation is developed by means of a mysterious statement which provokes misunderstanding on the part

of the questioner, and thus leads to the fuller elucida-
tion of the theme.   Such incidents show that the
author is much more interested in his message than
in the characters which flit across his pages.   We never
learn what happened to Nicodemus, who came to Jesus
by night.   When the teaching of the new birth has
been set forth fully, that ruler of the Jews has served
his purpose.   John has no more embarrassment in
offering an account of a private interview where there
were no witnesses than any modern dramatist.   Jesus
is even made to burst into a speech where there is no
audience at all.   The hand of the dramatist is seen
again in the account of the trial before Pilate.   The
vacillating Roman procurator is pictured as trotting
back and forth between the insistent high priests and
the majestic "king of truth."   John offers us not only
what went on in the street but also the words exchanged within the privacy of the palace.

Clement of Alexandria, at the beginning of the third
century, characterized the fourth Gospel as "the spiritual Gospel."   This designation has often been repeated without realizing what the ancient Greek
meant thereby.   For him, the spiritual meaning was
the allegorical meaning.   In addition to the literal
meaning of a passage we should seek also the allegorical significance.   There is certainly much allegory in
the fourth Gospel.   Instead of using parables, the
Johannine Jesus speaks such allegories as of the vine
and its branches, and the good shepherd who lays
down his life for his sheep.

Strictly speaking, no miracles are reported in the
fourth Gospel.   They are *signs*.   It is not the outward
wonder that matters but the inner significance of the
sign.   We shall never understand the turning of water

into wine at Cana of Galilee as long as we seek to find a moral justification for this contribution to the hilarity of a wedding party. The incident serves to illustrate that the wine of the Spirit which Jesus has to give is better than the water of purification which went before. It allegorizes the truth that the new is better than the old. Instead of pondering on what memories Lazarus might have brought back from the realm of the dead, we should recognize that this is a sign. Belief in Jesus means a present resurrection to life, not simply resurrection at the last day.

We are not to suppose that the author did not accept the literal accuracy of what he was reporting. Great marvels presented no difficulties in an age when there was no concept of a law-abiding universe. But from all of the wonders which he had heard reported from Jesus, he selected these seven because they were "signs" of the great truths which he sought to emphasize. His number symbolism is seen in his fondness throughout the Gospel for sevens. There are also seven "I am's" and seven witnesses to the faith in Christ.

Finally, we should look upon the fourth Gospel as *a book of devotion*. It reports primarily not what the eye saw, nor the ear heard, but what entered into the heart of man. The prologue is not an essay in theology. It is, rather, a three-stanza hymn to the creative divine Word, which had become flesh in Jesus. Throughout the Gospel we read the testimony of Christian experience. We may gain an entirely false impression of the attitude of Jesus from the fourth Gospel. A skeptic might easily come to think of him as a strutting egotist who was always talking about himself and making personal claims. He appears in a quite different light when we read these "I" words as the testimony of Christian experience. We should picture first the proclamation of the evangelist who asserts, "He is the Door; He is the Good Shepherd; He is the Way, the Truth, and the Life." The believing response comes back in adoration, "Thou art the Door; Thou art the Good Shepherd; Thou art the Way, the Truth, and the Life." Then a singer chants the words of divine revelation, "I am the Door; I am the Good Shepherd; I am the Way, the Truth, and the Life."

In the Gospel of John we feel ourselves in the midst of a worshiping congregation. We can almost see the elder lift the eucharistic bread toward heaven as he repeats the words, "This is the bread which cometh down out of heaven, that a man may eat thereof, and not die. . . . Except ye eat the flesh of the Son of man and drink his blood, ye have not life in yourselves." In these words we find joined the individual mystic and the devoted believer in the sacraments of the Church. John was both. Entrance into the Christian life was through both belief and baptism; our communion with Christ was through faith and the sacramental meal. The Johannine Christ prays for the unity of the Church, but it is in order that she may come into spiritual union with Christ and God. This great churchman has given us a book of devotion because he himself was a spiritual mystic, and that book has become the charter of Christian mysticism.

BOOKS FOR FURTHER STUDY

William Barclay, *The Gospel of John* (2 vols.).
Floyd V. Filson, *The Gospel According to John.*

SUGGESTIONS FOR THE STUDY OF JOHN

1. Many scholars believe that the text of John has suf-

fered several dislocations. The most common rearrangement of verses is followed in the modern translation by James Moffatt. It would be well to use this in your study.

2. Read the passages in which the Beloved Disciple and Peter are in competition: 13. 23f.; 18. 15f.; 19. 26; 20. 2.

3. As you read the Gospel, be on the lookout for hidden allegorical references other than those pointed out in the text of the chapter. For instance, do you think that in connection with the five porches of the pool of Bethesda (5. 2) there is any reference to the **five books of the Law** which had failed to bring healing?

4. The superiority of the *Revised Standard Version* and *The New English Bible* to the King James Version may be illustrated from this Gospel. Examine the margin notes on 5. 3-4 and 7. 53 to 8. 11. Remember that the first task of Biblical criticism is to determine what the text of the original author actually was.

5. Was 20. 31 the original conclusion of the Gospel? Note that the resurrection appearances in chapter 20 are all in Jerusalem, as in Luke. In chapter 21, they are all in Galilee, as in Matthew. Was the twenty-first chapter added to harmonize the two points of view and support the primacy of Peter?

6. As you read the Gospel try to form a description of what John means by eternal life. What is your own attitude toward John's reinterpretation of the teaching concerning Last Things (eschatology)?

7. Note in your reading how many specific moral commands you find. What do you learn from this as to the author's understanding of the Christian life? Is the fourth Gospel so popular because it makes so little of uncomfortable ethical demands?

8. Compare the controversies in Mark 2. 1 to 3. 6 with those in John 5, 7, and 8. Why should the themes be so different? Do you agree with the reason given in the chapter?

CHAPTER FIVE

THE MOST BEAUTIFUL GOSPEL—LUKE

IN the second century four Gospels were accepted as the basis for the faith of the Church. One of these, however, was originally written as the first volume of a history of Christianity. Before it could become part of the four-Gospel canon, the two volumes had to be separated. According to tradition, the author of this dual work was Luke, the beloved physician and companion of Paul. As far as the Gospel is concerned, there is no reason to doubt this ascription. Difficulties arise only with the second volume, which came to bear the title, "The Acts of the Apostles." We may postpone, therefore, until the next chapter a consideration of the question of authorship and simply use the name "Luke" to designate the writer of the two volumes dedicated to Theophilus.

In the opening preface Luke frankly states that he was dependent upon others for his information since he was not himself an eyewitness. Having made a careful investigation, he believed that he could improve upon the work of his predecessors. Some have pictured Luke taking advantage of the time of Paul's imprisonment in Caesarea to collect information about Jesus and the beginnings of the Church. In any case, he had access to new sources which are related to Samaria. The actual writing took place toward the close of the reign of Domitian (81-96). There is no unanimity of opinion as to the place. Like Matthew, Luke used Mark and the collection of sayings which we designate "Q." He also had an excellent special

58

source or sources which is usually referred to as "L." Some think that this contained another account of the Passion and was almost a Gospel in itself. Probably the birth stories came to Luke in documentary form, for they have a quite distinctive style.

The author of Luke was the greatest *literary artist* among the gospel writers. We can test his method in using his sources because Mark has been preserved for us. He frequently improves on the style, changing words and eliminating barbarisms. He was a Gentile with considerable background of culture and a wide vocabulary. At one time scholars believed that his occupation could be proved by his use of medical terms. It has been demonstrated, however, that the facts prove nothing more than that he was a man of wider culture than either Matthew or Mark. He was a born storyteller. We can never know how much of the art of the parable of the prodigal son is due to Jesus and how much to Luke.

Matthew and Luke had entirely different methods in using their documentary material. We have seen how Matthew joins together his sources and rearranges his material according to his own scheme. Luke follows one document at a time and apparently with almost never a change in order. Hence, there is little clarity to his outline. He uses the framework of Mark from 3. 1 to 9. 50. From 9. 51 to 18. 14 he strings together material from other sources under the guise of a journey through Samaria and Perea. From then on, the outline of Mark is again used, but with radical alterations in the Passion story, which may be due to the use of another source.

The *purpose* of Luke was, of course, the same as the other evangelists—to tell the gospel message. But the

very fact that he goes on to give an account of the
origins of the Church demonstrates his greater *historical* interest.   The man who begins his account of
the ministry of Jesus by naming the political and religious rulers of the period had a wider perspective than
Mark.   Judged by the standards of his time, Luke was
an excellent historian.   But he had far greater objec-
tives than merely recording facts.

There can be little doubt that he had a distinctively
political motivation.   Luke wrote at a time when the
official attitude toward the emergent Church was be-
coming more hostile.   He sought to show that in the
earlier period opposition had not come from Gentiles
but from Jews.   Four times he has Jesus pronounced
innocent by Gentile rulers.   Pilate finds no fault with
Jesus; Herod sends the prisoner back uncondemned;
twice more Pilate sought to release Jesus with only a
scourging.

The same thing is true in The Acts of the Apostles.
No Roman official is hostile when he has had a chance
to understand the situation.   It is the Jews who continually stir up the trouble.   Four times Gentile officials affirm that Paul has done nothing worthy of
death.   Claudius Lysias, Felix, Festus, and Herod
Agrippa all refuse to condemn Paul.   His final fate
must have been known to all Christians, but Luke
does not record the martyrdom.   Some have attempted
to account for this by dating Acts before the actual
death.   It has even been suggested that the book was
written for the defense of Paul at Rome.   This is un-
likely, for the Gospel of Luke uses Mark as a literary
source and it is impossible to date Mark within the
lifetime of Paul.   Nevertheless, the political purpose
of Luke in both writings is clear.

Writing as a Gentile, Luke is especially interested in the mission to non-Jews. In both volumes he tells how *the gospel was first rejected by the Jews and then carried to the Gentiles,* who accepted it. Each begins with a prophetic frontispiece to that effect. The rejection at Nazareth is moved to the beginning of the ministry of Jesus in order to typify his rejection by all of the Jews. Reference is made to the fact that in the past God's blessings had gone to Gentiles rather than to Jews. Luke shows throughout an interest in Samaritans, for they were the chief non-Jewish people with whom Jesus had contact. He had two versions of the missionary instructions of Jesus to the disciples. Instead of weaving them together as Matthew had done he transformed the second into a mission of seventy-two through Samaria. It should be remembered that according to contemporary beliefs this was the number of nations of the world. Luke puts the words of jubilation of Jesus at this point, for it was among the Gentiles that there was the greatest cause for rejoicing. When Luke tells the story of the great banquet, he adds an interesting touch. After the poor and the sick have been brought in from the streets of the city, the servants are sent again outside the city to constrain those in the highways to come in. He is thinking not only of the publicans and sinners, the neglected groups in Judaism, but also of the Gentiles who had responded to the summons for the Messianic banquet.

Though Luke may have been a companion of Paul, we must not suppose that he shared in the theology of the chief apostle to the Gentiles. The chief doctrine in his two books is not the death of Christ but his resurrection. That probably accounts for the strange

insistence throughout the close of Acts that Paul is
on trial for his belief in the resurrection. To Luke
that implied Christ's resurrection. For Paul, Christ
was the end of the law. For Luke, the law and the
gospel were not antithetical. Christianity was not a
new law, as in Matthew. Christianity was rather the
true Judaism. *All of the gospel was contained in the
law and the prophets if they were properly understood.* That is clearly the point of view of Luke.
Hence Father Abraham can say in the parable of the
rich man and Lazarus that it is sufficient to hear Moses
and the prophets. It was the function of the risen
Christ to interpret these Old Testament passages
aright to the disciples. Paul insists before Agrippa
that he says nothing but what the prophets and Moses
did say. The Jews at Rome are given the same assur-
ance. We see in the writings of Luke how some Gentiles held fast to the Old Testament because they read
their own faith back into its pages.

Yet, the Jesus of Luke is not a wooden automaton
fulfilling Scripture. He gives us the most human portrait of all. Jesus is seen as *the friend of publicans and
sinners.* Luke alone tells the story of the sinful woman
who washed the feet of the Lord. The setting for
the parables of the lost is the murmuring of the
Pharisees and the scribes, "This man receiveth sinners
and eateth with them."

Women have a new place of importance among the
followers of Jesus. Luke alone records how a group
of women ministered to the financial needs of Jesus
and his disciples. He alone tells the immortal incident of the visit to the home of Mary and Martha.
He alone tells of conversations between Elisabeth
and the mother of Jesus. An extraordinary number

of women are mentioned in The Acts of the Apostles —two Mary's, Dorcas, Lydia, Priscilla, Sapphira, Rhoda, the daughters of Philip, not to mention Drusilla and Bernice.

The Jesus of Luke is the *Saviour of the sick* in body and soul. In the two volumes are no less than four raisings from the dead. Miracles of healing were not looked upon as a special prerogative of Jesus, but in his name mighty deeds continue throughout the apostolic age. There is an element of tender sympathy which is distinctive of Luke's writing.

It is Luke who over and over again adds references to the *prayer life of Jesus* where it is not preserved by the other evangelists. Jesus is described as praying at baptism, on choosing his disciples, before his transfiguration, and before teaching his disciples to pray. Luke preserved more teaching about prayer than any of the other evangelists, especially of parables exhorting to persistence. It is the despised publican rather than a pious Pharisee who illustrates the contrite humility with which we must approach God.

We are indebted to Luke again for the preservation of some of the most precious of *the parables of Jesus.* If it were not for him, we would never have heard about a man who fell among thieves on the Jericho road. Except for his record, no Christian minister would ever have told the story of a young man who went into a far country and there wasted his substance in riotous living. We feel that the note of joy and gladness which pervades this beautiful Gospel must radiate much of the spirit of the Great Physician.

Luke had a special interest in *the Holy Spirit.* Despite his theory that the Spirit was first given at Pentecost, it is prominent throughout the birth stories in the Gospel. This matchless cycle is told with infinite tenderness. Along with the picture of the pious poor in Israel, he preserves several primitive Jewish-Christian psalms. The Magnificat and the Benedictus reflect something of their joy and hopes. Greater prominence is given to the Spirit in the min-, istry and teaching of Jesus than in the other Synoptic Gospels. It is in The Acts of the Apostles, however, that this interest comes into prominence. The Holy Spirit guides all of the development of the early Church. While Luke many times uses the phrase, "the kingdom of God," he no longer has keen interest in the coming of the new age. His stress is upon the gift of the Spirit which had come, rather than upon the eschatological kingdom of God which had not yet arrived.

The most prominent emphasis of Luke remains to be noted. He had a deeper *social interest* than any other evangelist and a profound sympathy for the poor. While very strong words against riches are preserved in the other early sources, it is to Luke that we must turn for the most severe condemnation of wealth. He takes the "poor" who are blessed in a strictly economic sense, and counterbalances the beatitude with a woe upon the rich. The man who lays up treasure on earth is simply a fool. No justification is offered for sending a rich man to future torment other than that he had enjoyed his good things in this life. Luke knows only one good thing to do with money, and that is to give it away in alms. Men should give without any thought of return. The same attitude toward possessions is revealed in the book of Acts. The generous sharing out of a new spirit of love is interpreted as if an actual community of goods had existed. Certainly that was Luke's ideal.

This social interest on the part of Luke is one of the major attractions of the Gospel to modern people, who give particular prominence to the human life of Jesus and the social task of the Church. The difference in point of view, however, should be clearly noted. In neither volume does Luke think of effecting changes in the economic order. Luke had very great sympathy for the poor, but he had no program for eliminating their poverty. He stressed the duty of almsgiving not to remove the curse of poverty, but to remove the spiritual peril of riches. It is not different in the Epistle of James where there is a similar exaltation of the poor and condemnation of riches. That author does not exhort men to social revolution, but to be patient until the Judgment. We must seek elsewhere for a program of economic change, but the inspiration to help the sick and the poor comes to the modern Christian more from the writings of Luke than from any other part of the New Testament.

BOOKS FOR FURTHER STUDY

William Barclay, *The Gospel of Luke*.
H. J. Cadbury, *The Making of Luke-Acts*.
Charles M. Laymon, *Luke's Portrait of Jesus*.

SUGGESTIONS FOR THE STUDY OF LUKE-ACTS

1. Some scholars believe that there was an earlier draft of the Gospel before Luke discovered Mark. This is designated Proto-Luke. Can you find passages that would have belonged in Proto-Luke?
2. Read in succession 1. 5-45 (drawn from a Hebraic

source), 5. 17-26 (adapted from Mark) and Luke's own composition in the preface, 1. 1-4. Do you perceive any differences in style?

3. Examine the following passages showing the political interest of Luke: 23. 4, 15, 20, 22. Acts 23. 29; 24. 23; 25. 25; 26. 31.

4. Read the following, showing Luke's interest in non-Jews: Luke 4. 16-30; 14. 15-24.

5. Observe Luke's emphasis on the resurrection: Acts 13. 33; 26. 23. Note that the Christian message is contained in the Old Testament: Luke 24. 44; Acts 26. 22; 28. 23.

6. Read the four accounts of raisings from the dead: Luke 7. 11-17; 8. 49-56; Acts 9. 39-42; 20. 9-12. Do you find any significance in the number of such accounts in Luke-Acts?

7. Study the prayer life of Jesus and his teaching on prayer: 3. 21; 6. 12; 9. 28; 11. 1-13; 18. 1-14.

8. Compare the story of the Passion in Luke with that in Mark. Note the new words at the Last Supper, the changed time of the hearing before the Sanhedrin (22. 66), the incident of Herod, and new words from the cross. Note that 23. 34 is not found in some of the ancient Greek manuscripts and may not be an original part of the Gospel.

9. On the social interest of Luke read 6. 20-24, 34-35; 12. 13-21; 16. 1-13, 19-26; Acts 2. 44-45; 4. 34-37. Do you think that Luke has exaggerated Jesus' attitude toward the poor?

CHAPTER SIX

THE FIRST HISTORY OF CHRISTIANITY— THE ACTS OF THE APOSTLES

THE second volume of Luke's story of the rise of Christianity was given the title "The Acts of the Apostles" when it came to circulate alone. It is a very poor description of its contents. Of the original Twelve whom Jesus sent out, only Peter occupies a prominent place in its pages. John is his shadow on numerous occasions, but the others are mere names. Luke tells how the place of Judas was filled, but nothing is reported of Matthias to confirm the decision of the Holy Spirit. Though later ecclesiastical legend attempted to supply this lack of information about the Twelve, little of it can be accepted as trustworthy. In Luke's story it is others who occupy the prominent place. Stephen is the first martyr; Philip, the evangelist, is the first bearer of the good news to Samaritans; Barnabas takes charge of the first mission to Greeks; and even at Jerusalem, James, the brother of Jesus, comes to the primacy at an early period.

A more accurate title might be *"The Acts of Peter and Paul,"* for these two figures dominate its pages. Luke does not tell us how the first disciples came to Damascus, Ephesus, or Rome. He tells how Paul reached these cities. As the story unfolds, there is a curious parallelism between the two chief figures. Both heal lame men, both invoke miraculous divine punishment, both are favored with providential escapes from prison, and both restore life to the dead. To Peter, the apostle to the circumcision, is assigned the honor of preaching the first sermon to a Gentile, and Paul's work in Jewish synagogues has a prominence which we would never suspect from his letters. So striking is this series of facts that it was once believed that a major objective in Acts was to reconcile the opposing factions of Peter and Paul.

But even concerning his heroes, Luke's story is very *fragmentary*. According to 12. 17, Peter goes "to another place," and that is the last we hear of him, except for the story of the apostolic Council in chapter 15. There is no valid reason to doubt that he made extensive missionary travels and later went to Rome, but Luke leaves us uninformed. Paul tells us that he had preached as far as Illyricum, but Luke leaves it out or does not know it. The apostle says that he was shipwrecked three times, thrice beaten with rods, and five times received thirty-nine stripes at the hands of Jews. Acts records only a fraction of these hardships.

This raises the question of *the identity of the author*. Was he Luke, the beloved physician and companion of Paul? Serious difficulties arise only in connection with the story of Paul. For the earlier period, Luke would have been dependent on the traditions which he could collect in Jerusalem, Caesarea, and Antioch. We would naturally expect gaps and discrepancies. But what of the career of Paul? Whoever wrote Acts was unfamiliar with the letters of Paul. Luke need not have seen the letters, but he must have known the main facts of Paul's life with some accuracy. Can the disputes over circumcision and table fellowship between Jew and Gentile as told in Galatians 2 be reconciled with the story in Acts? Did Paul act and speak as the vacillating trimmer on his last journey to Jerusalem as in Acts 21-23?

Some scholars think that these and other difficulties can be satisfactorily explained. Others hold that the final author must be a later figure who used a travel diary of a companion of Paul as one of his sources. This theory is entirely possible. While there is no difference in style between the sections written in the first person ("we-sections") and the rest of the book, the author might have edited this source just as we know that he edited Mark in the Gospel. The retention of the first person would not be unusual. The memoirs of Nehemiah were embodied by the author of Chronicles in his history of the Jews without changing the personal pronouns. It is too complex a problem to be discussed adequately within the limits of this chapter. We shall continue to designate the author as Luke without presuming to decide upon his identity. In either case the book is to be dated about 90 A. D.

Acts is of tremendous value in giving a picture of the first age of the Church. Its light may be dim at many places, but from the point at which it ends we are plunged into almost total darkness. Luke's geographical and historical information was excellent. At Philippi Paul meets with lictors; moving on to Thessalonica, he is dealt with by politarchs; at Athens he finds philosophers and is brought before the Areopagus; at Corinth, Gallio is described as the proconsul, and that provides a definite point of contact with world history; at Ephesus the official is the town clerk. In every case Luke is accurate in his terminology for the political officials of the city. Nevertheless, it is a grave disservice to attempt to prove the infallibility of Luke. There is no denying that his story bristles with difficult problems.

At the outset, we are told that the disciples did not leave Jerusalem but were commanded to wait for the Spirit, which was finally given fifty days after the crucifixion. Mark assumes, on the contrary, that the disciples fled back to Galilee, and the first resurrection appearances were there, according to Matthew. John asserts that Jesus sent the Spirit at once, not first after fifty days. Clearly, the early Christian traditions were not unanimous on these questions. If Luke is mistaken on these points, as many scholars believe, Pentecost is given much greater prominence in Acts than history would warrant.

Without any preparation, we are plunged in chapter 6 into a division between Hebrew and Hellenist believers. Luke says that seven were elected to serve tables in order to save the time of the apostles for missionary service. But at once they appear as flaming preachers of a more liberal message. A host of questions emerge which the historian would like to have answered, but we must remember that Luke was doing the best he could with the fragmentary traditions at hand. If anyone has ever tried to gather historical information about his own church, where full records have not been kept, he will sympathize with the difficulty of Luke's task. It is highly probable that in chapters 1-15 there are some doublets where he has given parallel versions of the same events. We know that in Genesis two different stories of the Flood are placed side by side. In places Luke seems to have included two versions of the same event, and the actual order of events was probably somewhat different.

Almost from the moment of his conversion Paul occupies the center of the stage. Beginning with chapter 16, the book is so exclusively his story that some have contended that it was written for his defense in the trial at Rome. It is customary to speak of *four missionary journeys,* but we prefer a somewhat different division than used to be given. (1) The earliest period included work in Damascus, Jerusalem, Tarsus, and Antioch. Paul's letters lead us to add Arabia, Syria and Cilicia, and cast doubt on the preaching in Jerusalem. (2) There followed a campaign with Barnabas and John Mark through Cyprus and southern Asia Minor which is described in chapters 13-14. While Acts assigns the break with Barnabas to a dispute over taking Mark again, Galatians gives a much more serious reason. They no longer saw eye to eye on the question of table fellowship between Jews and Gentiles. From this point on, Antioch is no longer Paul's base. Jerusalem never was a center for Paul, the Christian. He appears to be isolated by his radical stand on the law and only wins out by his enormously fruitful missionary work in the West. (3) A campaign through Macedonia and Achaia accompanied by Silas and Timothy is followed by a protracted stay in Corinth. (4) The final campaign centered in Ephesus with Titus and Timothy as his chief helpers, though the former is strangely never mentioned in Acts. It was followed by another trip through Macedonia and Greece to wind up the work in the East preparatory to proceeding through Rome to Spain. Acts ends, however, with the seizure in Jerusalem and the long story of the trial and trip to Rome. The collection, which we know held such a prominent place in Paul's mind during this period, is dismissed in one subordinate sentence.

No satisfactory explanation of *the ending of Acts* has ever been given. Some have thought that Luke

intended to write a third volume, but was prevented
or it was lost. An interesting new theory suggests
that if Paul stayed two years in his own hired house
without disturbance, the original readers would know
that the case must have automatically been dropped
under a statute of limitations. If Luke was not the
author, it may be that the writer's information was
exhausted. Many think that the death of Paul is pre-
supposed in the description of the last journey during
which Paul is constantly warned of impending disaster. We have no real knowledge that Paul was ever
released. Modern reconstructions to that effect are
based on the desire to find a place for the letters to
Timothy and Titus.

Luke follows a certain *stereotyped outline* in telling the story of Paul's missionary work in each city.
He recounts the beginning, which is in the synagogue
wherever possible. In other words, Paul sought out
those who had the greatest preparation for his message. Usually, Luke states where Paul stayed. This
interest in lodgings is curious. It may have arisen
out of the need of knowing the name of a prominent
church member in each city where traveling evangelists might spend the night. Then Luke tells the
source of opposition. Except at Ephesus, where busi-
ness connected with idolatry is involved, it always
comes from the Jews. No opportunity is lost to describe the friendliness of Roman officials. Outside
of an occasional anecdote and quite general descriptions of results, this is all that Acts has to tell us about
the development of the mission.

Just as striking is *what Luke omits*. We have no
hint of numbers in connection with the Pauline mission. For the Jerusalem church, figures are given

which are suspiciously large, but we have no means of knowing how many believers might be found in Berea or Ephesus. No insight is given into the difficulties involved in making Christian saints out of the former Gentiles who were baptized into the name of Jesus. Luke does not mention the strife and dissension in the church at Corinth, nor would we have ever learned of the disaffection of the churches in Galatia except through Paul's letters. No one would dream from Acts that Paul had any such clash with Peter as is described in Galatians 2. 11ff.

Luke does not fail, however, to record *the missionary message*. Except for Stephen's speech in Chapter 7, which stands apart as a piece of early Christian apologetic, Luke was probably responsible himself for the wording of these sermons. They are all much too short to be more than abstracts of what was said. All give much the same teaching. There is skillful adaptation to such different audiences as Jerusalem crowds, the household of Cornelius, an Antiochian synagogue, Athenian intellectuals, and King Agrippa, but none reveals a distinctive theology.

What is presented is *the essential apostolic message* in all of its simplicity. The one God who created heaven and earth had pronounced Jesus as his final messenger through the resurrection from the dead. There will be salvation at the coming Judgment only through his name. With Jews this is presented as the fulfillment of their own Scriptures. At Athens the point of contact is made with Stoic writings. This is an interesting revelation of missionary technique. Though Luke has told much of the teaching of Jesus in his Gospel, his second volume shows clearly that the apostolic message was not a repetition of this except with regard to the coming Judgment and the kingdom of God. What the apostles proclaimed was a message about Jesus—what God had done for men through him. There can be little doubt that Luke has preserved the essence of this message even though the wording is frequently his own.

From the standpoint of the religious teacher, it may appear strange that a book like The Acts of the Apostles is included in our New Testament. Learning the facts about Paul's journeys is not education in religion. Its presence reminds us, however, that Christianity is *a historical religion*. Our faith does not deal with timeless truths, but an act of God in history. It is not a religion which has sprung full-grown like Athena from the head of Zeus. There has been constant development from the days when the Jewish believers in the Messiahship of Jesus found their way to a truly universal religion, under the leadership of the Holy Spirit. The Acts of the Apostles tells the story of the first stages of that development. As we read its pages we should remember that it is a development which has gone on down the centuries. It is a development which goes on even in our own day.

BOOKS FOR FURTHER STUDY

William Barclay, *The Acts of the Apostles.*
Edward P. Blair, *The Acts and Apocalyptic Literature.*
F. J. Foakes-Jackson, *The Acts of the Apostles* (Commentary on the Moffatt translation).

SUGGESTIONS FOR THE STUDY OF ACTS

1. Read through the "we-sections": 16. 10-17; 20. 5-15; 21. 1-18; 27. 1 to 28. 16. Do you think that the origi-

nal diary must have been more extensive? Do other parts of Acts come from it?

2. Note Luke's interest in lodgings: Acts 16. 15; 17. 6; 18. 3; 21. 8; 21. 16.

3. Read Acts 3-4 and then chapters 2 and 5. Note how many facts and incidents are repeated twice. Do we have doublets here?

4. Note that 8. 4 and 11. 19 are contemporaneous. What bearing does this have on the chronology of the early period? Did the story of Cornelius actually come earlier than the events at Antioch?

5. Compare Acts 15 and Galatians 2, if possible with the help of a commentary. Paul's letters betray no knowledge of such a decree as is described in 15. 20. What bearing do the problems dealt with here have upon our attitude toward different races and toward Christian internationalism?

6. Trace carefully the four periods of Paul's missionary activity as outlined in the chapters: (1) 9. 20-30; 11. 25-30; (2) 13-14; (3) 16. 1 to 18. 17; (4) 18. 18 to 20. 4.

7. Read in turn the summaries of the early Christian sermons: 3. 12-26; 10. 34-43; 13. 16-41; 17. 22-31; 26. 2-23. What common elements of the gospel message do you find in these? To what extent is the gospel for today a different message? Whence do these differences arise?

8. What suggestions for modern missionary work do you find in Luke's story?

CHAPTER SEVEN

THE LETTERS OF A MISSIONARY

THE earliest Christian writings which have come down to us are the letters of Paul. All of our Gospels were written after his death. While the Gospels deal with events in the life of Jesus, they presuppose a more developed Church than Paul knew. Probably the only writings which we have from the first Christian generation are his letters.

Paul did not intentionally seek to create a Christian literature. Separated from the infant churches which he had organized, he needed to keep in touch with their problems. The writings are simply an extension of the voice of the missionary. Traditionally they have been called "Epistles." An epistle, however, is a public document in letter form. Paul did not write open letters, but intimate words of counsel, which were originally intended only for the ears of the readers. That they would ever become Holy Writ was certainly far from his imagination.

It was his custom to dictate his letters to an amanuensis. Since it was expected also that they would be read aloud to the church, it is well to study them by reading them aloud. We may picture Tertius, or some other scribe, sitting with a papyrus roll on his knee, and writing as Paul paces the floor. Doubtless he gesticulates with his hands, speaking now rapidly, and now slowly as he strives for the clearest expression of his thought. It is interesting to conjecture where pastoral interruptions may have come, and where dictation was resumed again. We wonder how

76

thoroughly Paul edited the work of his amanuensis.
At least it was his custom to close every letter with a
word in his own handwriting.

The reception of the letter also captivates our imagination. What a thrill it must have been to meet with
the company of handworkers, freedmen, and slaves,
who gathered at Corinth for their common meal,
which meant a participation in the body and blood
of Christ! As you enter the room you note a buzz of
extraordinary excitement. A letter has come from
Paul, and it will be read to the church that evening.
Think what it would have meant to hear the leader
read for the first time, "If I speak with the tongues of
men and of angels, but have not love, I am become as
sounding brass and a clanging cymbal." We may be
sure that it was put away in the most precious archives
of the little community and as other letters came, they
were preserved with it.

We do not know with certainty who first conceived
the idea of making *a collection* of all of the letters of
Paul which could be found. Doubtless before that,
there was an exchange of letters between individual
churches. But the various letters did not circulate
separately. Someone made a collection (probably of
ten letters) before the end of the first century. Their
publication and dissemination was an event of enor-
mous influence upon the later life of the Church.
Some believe that this collection took place at Corinth,
which furnished the largest amount of material. Other
indications point toward Ephesus. It is an interesting conjecture that the writing of The Acts of the
Apostles increased the interest in Paul and led to the
collecting of his extant writings.

Once collected, the Pauline letters formed the most

important body of apostolic writing which the Church possessed. Their right to a place in any Christian canon of Scripture was apparent. There may have been other Christian missionaries whose labors rivaled those of Paul in importance. But no figure in the apostolic Church could compare with him in later influence, for none other left such a written record of his faith.

The letters follow certain *stereotyped forms*. First came the name of the author. Paul frequently associated others with himself in the address, but we may be sure that he alone is responsible for the contents. The recipients are then named with not only the city or region addressed, but some description of their Christian status. There follows the salutation, which is uniformly of "grace and peace" from God and Christ. Next in order is a thanksgiving for mercies either to Paul or the church addressed. Only once is that omitted; Paul had nothing to be thankful for in the churches of Galatia. In First Corinthians the thanksgiving is decidedly ironical. While this was a formal part of the letter, we must not think that it was a mere form. It is amazing how frequently and naturally Paul is led to speak of his own prayers.

The *close of the letter* had also its standing formulas. There are greetings from companions of Paul, and sometimes greetings to particular readers. It is interesting to note, however, that the last occur only in the letters to the two churches which Paul had not yet visited—Rome and Colossae. He was never so tactless as to pick out individuals for greetings in the communities where he was personally known to all. He closed with a short benediction, usually the simple words—"The grace of our Lord Jesus Christ be with you."

The structure of the *body of the letter* was, of course, determined by the particular purpose. On the whole, however, he followed the practice of treating first questions of a more doctrinal character, and then to give practical moral exhortations. Sometimes these were determined by the particular problems of that church; at other times they were general advices applicable to all Christians. Because they were genuine letters, some parts of the Pauline correspondence are obscure to us. They all presuppose his missionary message, which none of us has heard. They deal with problems with which the original readers were perfectly familiar, but we must read the situation between the lines as best we can. It should be especially borne in mind that Paul did not write to give a system of Christian doctrine. He would have been amazed to think of later preachers spending a half hour discoursing on a single sentence which he had casually dictated to his amanuensis. Though certain parts may have been independently composed with considerable care, we should never forget that we are dealing with the correspondence of a missionary, not the creedal formulations of a theologian.

Because we possess these intimate letters, *we know Paul as we know few figures of antiquity*. The psalm-like passages show to what heights of expression he could rise. The illustrations of rabbinic dialectic confirm our knowledge of his experience in the schools of Judaism. He also utilizes the device of the Stoic-cynic diatribe by expressing his point through imaginary dialogue with a hypothetical opponent. His loving friendliness breathes through every page, even when he is lashing out against those whom he believes to be mistaken.

It is dangerous to attempt to trace a development of thinking on the basis of the letters which we have. The earliest was written in 49-50 A. D. Paul had already been a Christian for more than fifteen years and had come to full maturity of thinking. All of our letters come from the following ten years. The very real differences between the thought of the letters is much more due to changing needs and circumstances than to any marked change of his own understanding of the Christian faith. In the balance of this chapter we shall deal briefly with the letters to Thessalonica and Corinth, reserving for the next a study of the rest of the letters attributed to him.

Thessalonica was an important center in the province of Macedonia. From Acts we learn that Paul's work there was cut short by the hostility of the Jews. He went on to Berea, Athens, and finally to Corinth, where conditions were favorable for an extended missionary campaign. But his spirit was deeply troubled all the while concerning the church at Thessalonica. Finally, Timothy brought back to him reassuring words, but apparently also information about problems calling for attention.

First Thessalonians is a simple, direct letter with brief references to his missionary message, heartfelt expressions of love, but especially words about *the coming of Christ* which would bring the end of the age. The readers are assured that the friends who had died would not thereby lose their part in the coming salvation. Those who live should find in the coming of Christ a tremendous motivation to righteous living.

Apparently, this stress on the coming age produced

results which were not altogether pleasing to Paul.
Second Thessalonians must have been written very
shortly thereafter. From it we learn that some of the
members of the church had stopped work and were act-
ing as busybodies. Paul hastens to remind them that
the end could not come before a series of expected
signs had taken place. The man of lawlessness must
first appear, but now there was one who restrained
him. Paul points to his own practice of never living
at the expense of the community, but working hard
with his own hands. The Thessalonians should practice the same sober diligence. When Paul wrote, "If
any will not work, neither let them eat," he was not
thinking of the unemployed in a machine civilization
but the religious fanaticism which had unfortunately
followed his message.

The Corinthian correspondence is of much greater
permanent interest. The church at this crossroads of
the Mediterranean resulted from eighteen months of
labor in the province of Achaia. From there Paul
transferred his headquarters to Ephesus, where he
worked for more than two years. First Corinthians
was written from there and Second Corinthians after
leaving for Macedonia. The letter which we call First
Corinthians, however, was not the first to that community, for in it Paul refers to an earlier communica-
tion giving advices which had been misunderstood.
It concerned a revolting case of incest, and Paul is
demanding the severe punishment of the offending
member of the church.

But there were many other reasons for writing to
Corinth. Word had come through the slaves of Chloe
that *factions* had arisen between followers of the different leaders, Apollos, Cephas, and Paul. Paul decries

such a spirit of factionalism, and also believes that certain teachings which were being propagated were destructive in character. Furthermore, the Corinthians themselves had sent a letter *inquiring about certain problems*. We should remember that there was no public post, and all of Paul's letters had to be carried by friends such as Stephanas and others. The subjects of inquiry are introduced by a stock phrase, "now concerning" things sacrificed to idols, concerning spiritual gifts, marriage, the resurrection, and the collection which Paul was taking for the poor saints in Jerusalem.

We have in this letter the most *intimate window into the life of a Gentile church* of the first century. It reveals how many phrases had been adopted from the mystery religions of the time; it shows the stern ethical demands of the new Christian faith, calling especially for purity of sexual living. There is the demand for consideration for the weaker members of the community who could not yet fully act on the conviction that there was only one God. Food sacrificed to idols seemed dangerous even though they were assured that an idol was nothing. We see intimate pictures of their worship, where ability to speak in tongues was so greatly overvalued. Paul exalted prophecy instead, but above all such "gifts" of the Spirit stood love. And, lastly, we have the earliest accounts both of the Last Supper and of the appearances of the risen Christ. Paul was led to recount these traditions because of disorders in the common meal, and the difficulty which his Greek readers had in the idea of the resurrection of the body. How much more information about Jesus might Paul have given us if there had been a particular reason?

But this letter did not settle the problems of that church. It is apparent from Second Corinthians that Paul had to make a visit to the community between these writings. Also, another letter, written "in tears and anguish," intervened. Many scholars find a part of this in chapters 10-13 of Second Corinthians. The irony and invective of those chapters do stand in strange contrast to the spirit of reconciliation in the early part. It is altogether probable that our Second Corinthians is a transcription to one roll of portions of several of Paul's letters.

Second Corinthians is one of the most auto-biographical of our collection. We see Paul defending his authority as an apostle, the integrity of his mission, and the truth of his message. We see him subject to slander, vilification, and misrepresentation, yet radiant in faith, and hope, and love. We do not understand fully every allusion which is made, but it is *an open window into the life of Paul,* just as First Corinthians is a portrait of an early Christian community. To read these books with imagination is to live again in the apostolic age.

BOOKS FOR FURTHER STUDY

F. W. Beare, *St. Paul and His Letters.*
William R. Cannon, *Journeys After St. Paul.*
Morton S. Enslin, *Letters to the Churches.*

SUGGESTIONS FOR THE STUDY OF PAUL

1. Examine the opening and closing of several of the letters of Paul to verify the structure described in the chapter.
2. 2 Corinthians 6. 14 to 7. 1 is sometimes assigned to the lost first letter to Corinth. What reasons do you find for or against that conclusion?
3. How would you judge the ethical progress of the

Church from 1 Thessalonians 4. 1-8? Why were such elementary injunctions necessary?

4. Read 2 Thessalonians 2. 1-10. This is a little "apocalypse." Both "the man of lawlessness" and "the one who restrains" are probably mythological figures which were part of Paul's Jewish inheritance.

5. Compare Paul's description of "last things" in 1 Thessalonions 4. 15-17 with 1 Corinthians 15. 20-28. Should we try to harmonize such pictures into literal predictions of future events? Notice that Paul expected to live to the end (1 Corinthians 15. 51).

6. If you know any church beset by divisions, read 1 Corinthians 1-4. What principles does Paul lay down? Are they still valid and useful?

7. Read the discussion of meat sacrificed to idols in 1 Corinthians 8-10. Do you find any applicability to the question of the use of intoxicants today?

8. On what does Paul base his appeal for gifts for his great collection? See 2 Corinthians 8-9. What application do you find for modern church finance?

9. Read of Paul's "thorn in the flesh" (2 Corinthians 12. 7-10). Was his prayer answered? It is not certainly known what this malady was, though many believe that it was epilepsy.

CHAPTER EIGHT

THE FAITH OF PAUL

THE first written expressions of Christian faith were the missionary letters of Paul. In the previous chapter we reviewed the conditions under which they were written and sought to understand the purpose of the letters to Thessalonica and Corinth. Here we shall survey the rest of his letters in order to draw from them a clearer understanding of the faith of the apostle.

We have a good introduction in the letter to the Galatians, for that document proclaims emancipation from the trammels of national Judaism. It is a brilliant affirmation *of Christian freedom*. The crisis which provoked the letter is clear. The churches of Galatia had joyously received the gospel from Paul. After his departure other teachers had come and unsettled their faith. They insisted that Paul was not a genuine apostle. They asserted that the only way in which Gentiles could inherit God's promises to Abraham was through acceptance of the rite of circumcision and obedience to the Law.

Though the general situation is clear, there is no agreement among New Testament scholars as to where those Galatian churches are to be found, or when the letter was written. Formerly it was assumed that they were to be found in Galatia proper, a region in the heart of Asia Minor. Luke, however, tells nothing of the founding of churches here. Hence it is popular today to identify them with the churches founded on the campaign with Barnabas, that is, Lystra, Derbe,

Iconium, and Antioch. These cities belonged to the Roman province of Galatia at this time, though their inhabitants were not Galatians. When this latter theory is accepted, the letter is sometimes held to be the earliest from Paul. Most, however, believe that it was written either from Corinth after Thessalonians, or from Ephesus after First Corinthians.

Paul had visited the readers at least twice. He defends himself vehemently against the accusations which have been made, and in so doing gives an invaluable summary of his conversion, early ministry, and defense of his Gentile mission at a meeting with the "pillars" of the Jerusalem church. We have noted in Chapter Six that it is not easy to harmonize this testimony with the story in The Acts. Naturally, Paul's own word should be given the preference for he is here practically speaking under oath as he sets forth the independence of his Law-free gospel.

The details of the argument in Galatians may not appeal to the average Bible reader of today. He may agree with Paul that the essence of Christianity is faith, but he will probably not see any importance in being a child of Abraham. We must put ourselves back into the original situation where the readers had been unsettled by the Jewish-Christian agitators. Furthermore, we must never forget that if Paul had not successfully maintained the freedom of the Gentile Christians, we ourselves should probably never have heard of the gospel message. Galatians is also *a permanent protest against any reversion to a legalistic interpretation of Christianity.* "For freedom did Christ set us free . . . be not entangled again in a yoke of bondage." But Christian liberty never meant to Paul a liberty to sin. If men were freed from an obligation to keep the Jewish Law, it was to enable them to walk by the Spirit. The fruit of the Spirit was love, joy, kindness, faithfulness, and self-control. Against these there was no law, and what was more, no law could ever produce them.

Galatians was struck off at white heat in the midst of a terrific struggle against the Judaizers for the validity of his interpretation of Christian faith. We do not know whether the letter succeeded in its purpose. At a later time Paul drew up a more dispassionate statement of his interpretation of the relationship of Christianity to Judaism. This is to be found in his letter to the Romans. As Paul prepared to wind up his work in the East and to turn westward to Spain, he wrote his most elaborate letter to the world metropolis introducing himself and setting before them *the nature of his gospel.* Naturally, this is a much more formal document than the ones which we have hitherto considered, for Paul was not writing to his own converts. While it has not been especially popular with the average Bible reader, it has exercised crucial influence on such leaders as Augustine and Luther.

The body of the letter falls into three parts. In the first eight chapters Paul shows how man was in desperate need as a sinner until *God had provided deliverance through Christ.* The Law had been powerless to meet such an adversary as "the flesh." Only as men accept God's deliverance through faith can they be pronounced righteous in his sight (justified). This faith brings union with Christ through baptism, and makes us possessors of the Spirit, through which we may be victorious over all adversaries. Beside the thirteenth of Corinthians stands the eighth of Romans

as the two greatest inspirations from the pen of Paul.
Here, and not in the story of Pentecost, is the true
Christian conception of the Spirit. The chapter closes
with the triumphant confession, "I am persuaded, that
neither death, nor life, nor angels, nor principalities,
. . . nor any other creature shall be able to separate
us from the love of God, which is in Christ Jesus our
Lord."

In the second section (chapters 9-11), Paul deals
with *the fate of his own people*. How could it be that
God had cast off the Jews? We should realize that at
the time of the writing of this letter (ca. 55 A. D.) it
was already apparent that the Jews as a whole would
never accept the Christian message. Paul explores
the solution of predestination in chapter 9, of free will
in chapter 10, and various mediating possibilities in
chapter 11. Finally he takes refuge in the unsearch-
able wisdom and mercy of God. The Gospel of John
accepts without apparent regret the fact that the
"Jews" had not been drawn to Christ by the Father;
but Paul writes out of deep anguish of soul for the
fate of his own people.

The ethical advices comprise the third section, extending from 12. 1 to 15. 13. We cannot tell whether
these are typical Pauline exhortations, or whether he
had learned of the existence of differences over Sab-
batarianism and vegetarianism in the Roman church.
His tribute to the political power of Rome reveals
clearly that he did not look upon Christianity as a
revolutionary movement. "The powers that be are
ordained of God." The salvation that was near was
not to come through revolution; it was the new age
which God himself would send. But this deliverance
which we receive by faith did not make ethical en-

deavor unnecessary. "I beseech you therefore, brethren, by the mercies of God, to present your bodies a living sacrifice, holy, acceptable to God, which is your spiritual service."

There are many difficult *critical problems* associated with Romans which we cannot attempt to examine here. The word "Rome" is missing from some of our most ancient manuscripts, and there is evidence that some manuscripts stopped with either the fourteenth or fifteenth chapter. Apparently, this most formal statement of Paul's faith circulated at some time as an encyclical letter. Many scholars believe that chapter 16 is no part of the original letter of Paul. They think that it is improbable that he could know twenty-six individuals by name in a church which he had never visited. Certainly, some of the names would fit well at Ephesus. Hence it has often been held that chapter 16 is a note of introduction for Phoebe addressed by Paul to Ephesus at the same time that Romans was written.

Philippians, Colossians, Philemon, and Ephesians are joined together by the fact that they were all written from prison. Formerly it was debated whether that was in Caesarea or Rome. It has been shown, however, that Paul may have suffered an earlier imprisonment in Ephesus, unreported in Acts. Some would assign one or more of these letters to this time. I still think that it is more probable that the first three at least were written from Rome.

Philippians is a "Thank-you" letter for a contribution which had been brought by Epaphroditus from this favorite Macedonian church. Its keynote is *joy*. Though he was faced by the jealousy of others, and the confinement of his bonds, the veteran apostle exclaims, "Rejoice in the Lord always." One of the most important passages of the letter is the hymn in the midst of exhortations to lowliness at the beginning of the second chapter. It does not present any illustrations of humility from the earthly life of Jesus, but the condescension of the heavenly Being who came to earth. In contrast to the first Adam who had been cast out of the garden of Eden for his disobedience, this second Adam took the form of a servant and was obedient even unto the death on the cross. In the third chapter we also have an important biographical passage. The former Pharisee had to turn his back upon all which had been precious to him in order to gain Christ. He is now pressing on toward the future consummation, but with peace and contentment in his heart.

The theme of Colossians is *the supremacy of Christ*. Paul had never visited this little town up the Lycus valley, but word had come to him of a crisis caused by a false philosophy. It was believed by certain teachers that there were many heavenly angelic powers in which the "fullness" of God dwelt. Hence it was important to worship these also. Apparently ascetic practices were likewise commended. Paul insists that *all* of the fullness of God dwelt in Christ. Hence none of these "elements of the universe" could do anything for us which Christ could not do. In fact, Paul goes so far as to claim that it was through Christ that the whole universe had been created by God, even the angels whom these teachers would have them worship.

We should note that Paul was induced to such flights of speculation by the very practical need which he was facing in the life of the Colossian church. The conclusion is definitely practical: to submit to such ordinances as "Handle not, nor taste, nor touch" is to return to the bondage of these lesser deities. Colossians contains some of the most beautiful expressions of *the mystical sharing in the sufferings of Christ.* "Now I rejoice in my sufferings for your sake, and fill up on my part that which is lacking of the afflictions of Christ in my flesh for his body's sake, which is the church. . . . Ye died, and your life is hid with Christ in God." This is also the first Christian document to contain a table of household duties. The prominence of injunctions to slaves is especially noteworthy.

Philemon is a personal note written at the same time as Colossians to an individual member of the church. It is *an appeal on behalf of the runaway slave,* Onesimus, whom Paul is returning to his master. The note, which could have been written on a single sheet of papyrus, reflects in a charming way the graciousness of Paul. Defenders of slavery made much of the fact that Paul sent Onesimus back to his master. Recent interpreters, however, are of the opinion that Paul was really asking Philemon to give this slave his freedom for an important piece of Christian service. That may be what is meant by "do even beyond what I say."

Ephesians is an Epistle concerning whose interpretation there is as yet no agreement. One thing alone is certain: it is not a letter of Paul to Ephesus. As the revised version indicates, the words "at Ephesus" are not found in the best manuscripts. It is impossible that Paul could have written to the church where he labored longest and say simply that he had "heard of their faith." Some scholars hold that it was an encyclical Epistle sent to a group of churches in Asia.

Others believe that it is the "letter from Laodicea" referred to in Colossians 4. 16.   Still others do not believe that these labored, involved sentences come from the pen of Paul himself, but, rather, from a later imitator who had immersed himself in Paul's ideas.   A recent conjecture is that the collector of Paul's letters wrote Ephesians as an introduction to the collection, basing it on Colossians, which he had known longest.

The theme of Ephesians is that of *unity*.   The mystery is no longer that of the indwelling Christ, as in Colossians, but the union of Jew and Gentile into one Church.   The message is not primarily that Christ has reconciled men to God through the sacrifice of his body on the cross.   It is that Jew and Gentile are reconciled through the mystical body of Christ which is the Church.   Nevertheless, the essential Pauline message is not lost: "By grace have ye been saved through faith."   And the stern note of ethical demand, so characteristic of Paul, is not lost in mystical ecstasy. One of the most stirring passages is where the Christian's warfare against the terrible powers of evil is depicted.   But the only weapons which Paul commends are righteousness, and faith, and prayer.

Three other letters bear the name of Paul, personal communications to Timothy and Titus.   No place can be found for them within the known life of Paul. The only way in which their genuineness can be defended is by assuming that Paul was released from his imprisonment at Rome and made another extensive trip through the East.   But the vocabulary and style are quite new, the problems are very different, and a much more advanced stage in the organization of the Church is assumed.   It is therefore the opinion of an increasing number of scholars that these letters, long called "the pastorals," were written at a later time when the authority of the great Apostle to the Gentiles was valuable in meeting new exigencies. Their actual background and message will be treated in Chapter Ten.

Only one question concerning these letters needs notice here. Were fragments of genuine notes of Paul included in them? Several passages containing personal items seem to bear the mark of genuineness. An examination of Second Timothy, where most of these occur, shows that they could hardly have come from the same situation. When a man is singing his swan song and expecting immediate martyrdom, we would not expect him to write for his library and his winter overcoat.

This chapter has been called "the faith of Paul." We must bear in mind, however, that we do Paul an injustice if we try to distill from these occasional letters anything like a systematic theology. They should be read as triumphant testimonies of faith, not as a rigid system for which we claim permanent validity. We value the letters of Paul today, not because we expect to share all of his ideas, but because we want to catch from him the inner significance of Christ for men.

BOOKS FOR FURTHER STUDY

William Barclay, *Flesh and Spirit.*
C. H. Dodd, *The Meaning of Paul for Today.*
James Stewart, *A Man in Christ.*

SUGGESTIONS FOR BIBLE STUDY

1. Try to fix in your mind a phrase descriptive of each of the letters of Paul dealt with in this chapter.
2. Read Galatians 3 as typical of the dialectic of Paul, and Romans 8 for a confident expression of his faith.

3. Examine the following passages for their bearing on an imprisonment of Paul at Ephesus: 2 Corinthians 1. 8ff.; 11. 23; Romans 16. 7.

4. Read through Philemon for its portrayal of the human qualities of Paul. What evidence do you find in the other letters of his capacity to make friends? Why should such a friendly man have had so many enemies?

5. Read the following for their bearing on Paul's speculation about Christ: Philippians 2. 6-11; Colossians 1. 13-20. Could all of these statements be a part of actual experience?

6. Compare "the table of duties" in Colossians 3. 18 to 4. 1 with Ephesians 5. 22 to 6. 9. These follow a pattern widely used in the Hellenistic world. What is there that is specifically Christian about these injunctions?

7. How can Paul's doctrine of salvation by faith only be made more meaningful to twentieth-century Christians? To what extent are we in danger of substituting works for dependence upon God's grace?

8. From what bondage do men need deliverance today? How does God bring *us* real deliverance through Christ?

9. It is sometimes held that Paul changed the simple faith of Jesus into a complicated theology. Others believe that Paul is the greatest interpreter of the meaning of Christ. Which do you think is true?

10. What relationship may exist between the use of terms found in Essene literature and those in Colossians?

CHAPTER NINE

ESTABLISHING THE FAITH OF THE CHURCH; EPISTLE, TRACT, AND HOMILY

THE first period of Christian history was *the Apostolic Age*. The term is used for the first generation of the Church, from the crucifixion (30 A. D.) to the fall of Jerusalem (70 A. D.) when Titus destroyed the Temple and the Jewish sacrifices ceased forever. We know many of the events of this period, because The Acts of the Apostles was preserved. It was marked by definite personalities such as Stephen and Barnabas, Peter and Paul, James and John. It was a time of rapid expansion over the Mediterranean world as men were driven by the power of a new enthusiasm to propagate their faith. But the only documents which have come down to us from this period are the letters of Paul, and the gospel of Mark written at its close. Creative leaders were too busy to write books.

The next forty or fifty years (70-115 A. D.) may well be designated *the critical period* of the Christian Church. The second and third generations faced the task of organizing and consolidating the movement. Since the Jews as a whole had definitely rejected the message, the new converts came from among the Gentiles. They had to be trained in the ethical standards of the new religion. A more exact formulation of the faith had to be stated in contrast to competing movements. The functions of ministerial leadership had to be worked out. The forms of worship had to be

adapted to growing experience. A fixed attitude had
to be adopted toward the State and the pagan society
which surrounded them. All of these problems must
be faced without the leadership of the dominating
personalities of the first age. It was not a period of a
few great minds, but, through the Spirit of God, many
lesser men made their contribution to the developing
Christian movement.

Within this period, all of the rest of the New Testament books were written, except Second Peter, which
it is universally conceded was written in the apostle's
name about 150 A. D. Second and Third John are
genuine letters of an authoritative elder, which deal
with problems of changing organization in Asia Minor.
The "elect lady" is a church which is warned against
wandering teachers, but in Third John the elder com-
plains to Gaius that his own emissaries have been rejected by a certain Diotrephes. We have already discussed the Gospels and The Acts in earlier chapters.
Revelation will be dealt with in Chapter Eleven.

The rest of the booklets may be described as epistles, tracts, and homilies. The so-called Catholic
Epistles are open letters to the Christian world as a
whole, in contrast to Paul's personal letters to individual churches. Some of them, however, are better
described as religious *tracts* or *written sermons*. In
the next chapter we shall deal with those books which
are devoted to defending the faith, primarily, the Epistle to the Hebrews. In this, we shall discuss three
books which, though known under apostolic names,
are now usually assigned to this later period.

The Epistle of James is addressed to "the twelve
tribes of the dispersion." Obviously, no postman
could deliver such a letter. What follows is a series

of moral exhortations by a servant of God who bore the name of James. It was accepted into the canon in the fourth century under the belief that it had been written by the brother of Jesus by that name. The book itself makes no such claim, however, and no writer in the second century quoted it as apostolic. It is clear that it was written in a later time when Paul's doctrine of justification by faith had led to excesses. James holds that salvation is by works rather than faith. He did not understand what Paul meant by faith, interpreting it simply as barren belief. For James, Christianity is not a religion of redemption. It is a new law, the royal law of liberty. Because of this radically different interpretation of Christianity, Martin Luther branded the book as "an epistle of straw." Though it is not a work of great genius, this is a very unjust description. It is true that the primitive enthusiasm of a Spirit-moved Church had cooled into a prosaic moralism. It contains little that is distinctively Christian, the name of Jesus appearing only twice. But it is eminently practical, filled with such admonitions as "Be ye doers of the word and not hearers only."

Sins of speech are among those most frequently attacked. The word against swearing is probably a more original form of the saying of Jesus than that in the Gospel of Matthew, "Let your yea be yea, and your nay, nay." Akin to Luke is his attitude toward wealth. But men of wealth are now in the Christian community itself leading to the danger of social distinctions. In words reminiscent of the Old Testament prophets James flays the economic injustice practiced by the rich. It does not lead him to a call for social revolution. Instead, believers are exhorted to wait patiently for the coming of the Lord, which would bring with it the overturning of the institutions of men.

The book which we call *First John* does not even have the form of a letter. It contains no indication of authorship except its obvious kinship to the fourth Gospel. As we have seen in an earlier chapter, that does not come directly from the apostle John. This little book enforces many of the same ideas as the Gospel. The particular occasion calling forth the sermon was the appearance of false teachers, which the author designates as antichrists. They did not believe that the man Jesus was the Christ of God. The real Christ had not appeared in actual flesh. This emergency accounts for the stress of the author upon an appearance which could be handled and seen. John insists that the Son of God was the Jesus who had been baptized with water and had died on the cross.

Apparently, these teachers did not sufficiently stress "love." After reading First John, we may wonder how much love its author had in his own heart for these "heretics." But he is insistent that belief in Christ called for ethical living. Just as in the Gospel of John, there are very few definite moral injunctions. Instead there is constant repetition of the same general themes. Communion with God is not possible apart from abiding in Christ. How do we abide in Christ? The answer is, By keeping his commandments. And what are his commandments? Only one is named, the new commandment of love. But love brings us back to communion with God. He is the one source of love. Without love, there is no knowledge of God, for he himself is love. Still, no one can love the God whom he has not seen unless he loves the brother whom he has seen. "Whoso hath the world's goods, and beholdeth his brother in need, and shutteth up his compassion from him, how doth the love of God abide in him?"

John likes to deal with *sharp and absolute contrasts*. Men either walk in light or in darkness; they either love or hate; they either belong to the truth or a lie, to God or the devil. He that believes must have no love for the world. That was soon to pass away, for the last hour was at hand. "But he that doeth the will of God abideth forever."

105454

Belief was for John more much intellectual than it was in Paul. It is from the Johannine writings that the Church received the idea that *faith consisted in holding correct opinions* about the person of Jesus. In evaluating that tendency we must remember the particular crisis which John faced. He did not fear that Christians would think of Jesus just as a man like unto themselves. The danger was that the heavenly Christ would be divorced from the historical Jesus. But we are thankful that he gave such pregnant expression unto the heart of the Christian faith: "Herein is love, not that we loved God, but that he loved us, and sent his Son *to be* the expiation for our sins. . . . We love, because he first loved us."

The apostolic authorship of *First Peter* is still maintained by some. The defenders have attempted to account for the undoubted influence from Paul on the theory that Peter had read several of the letters of Paul at Rome. That a Galilean fisherman should write such excellent Greek is explained as due to Silvanus, who is named as the emanuensis. In fact, some would say that Silvanus wrote in Peter's name.

The insuperable difficulty, however, is that the readers are suffering official *persecution for the sake*

of the Christian name. That this was the case within
the lifetime of Peter over all of Asia Minor is incredible. The only way in which the defenders can meet
this point is to claim that the letter presupposes nothing more than social persecution by neighbors. But
murderers and thieves are punished by the police, not
by irate neighbors. When confessing the name of
Jesus is mentioned alongside of these accusations, it is
clear that the author had State action in mind. Modern scholars are divided on the actual time of writing
between the end of the reign of Domitian (81-96) and
the reign of Trajan (98-117). Fortunately, the correspondence between Trajan and Pliny, the governoɪ
of Bithynia, has been preserved, which relates how
persecution for "the name" was actually carried on.
But we cannot be sure how much earlier the procedure had been followed.

It is a popular theory at the present time to hold
that most of First Peter (1. 2 to 4. 11) was a sermon
delivered to baptismal candidates by a prominent
Bishop. In this section, the problem of persecutions
is much less intense. It deals with the glorious hope
to which they had been begotten by the resurrection
of Jesus Christ. They had received the imperishable
seed of the "word of God" and were to be fed with the
spiritual milk and built up into a new spiritual house.

After the beautiful description of the salvation
which they had received, the author turns to his moral
advices. He follows the device of the "table of duties"
which we first met in Colossians. He begins with the
political duties. In contrast to Revelation, which was
also written in the midst of persecution, he calls for
subjection to the emperor. "Peter" insists that the
best way to meet opposition was through a good man-

ner of life. The actual Peter had died thus at the hands of Nero. The slaves receive the longest exhortations. Strikingly, their sufferings are compared with the sufferings which Jesus had borne on the tree. First Peter makes more of the example of Jesus than any other New Testament book, but it is only in connection with the necessity to suffer as he had suffered.

One of the most interesting incidental references in First Peter is to the belief that Jesus had gone to preach to the "spirits in prison." After the belief was formulated that it was on the third day that Christ had been raised from the dead, pious curiosity naturally came to ask what he had been doing in the intervening time. *"The descent into Hades"* was the most popular answer. The belief was incorporated into the Apostles' Creed, though John Wesley eliminated the clause for his societies because he felt that the idea was unchristian. "The spirits in prison," to which Peter refers, are probably the fallen angels; these and the Noah generation were just the ones which had no hope of salvation according to current Jewish belief. It is noteworthy that in this passage it is primarily these who receive the preaching message of Christ. Christian sensibilities have often found difficulty in accepting the idea that those who had no opportunity to know Christ should have no chance in all eternity. This tradition reveals the earliest wrestling with the problem in the form of the myth of the descent of the Saviour into the underworld.

This chapter has been called "Establishing the Faith of the Church." That was the purpose of the little books which we have surveyed. They were not written bv original theologians. They presuppose *a common body of faith.* The primary emphasis in each one is ethical and practical. It is instructive to note that this ethical teaching was not given in the form of "words of Jesus." Not one of the authors cites a moral advice on the authority of Jesus. He gives his exhortations on his own authority. Many of them are to be paralleled from the popular philosophy of the time and from Hellenistic Judaism. This practice shows clearly that Christianity did not mean following the teachings of Jesus. Christ was their Redeemer. The ethical problems of life had to be faced in the light of all of the wisdom that could be found in the contemporary world. Not all of their conclusions satisfy us today, but the point of view of these writings helps us to formulate a Christian attitude in the modern world.

BOOKS FOR FURTHER STUDY

E. J. Goodspeed, *An Introduction to the New Testament.*

James Moffatt, *The General Epistles* (Commentary on the Moffatt translation).

SUGGESTIONS FOR BIBLE STUDY

1. What might lead to the inclusion into the canon of such small letters as Second and Third John?
2. Compare the attitude of James 1. 27 and John 2. 15-17 toward "the world" with that of modern Christians. How do you account for the difference?
3. Read James 3. 1-12 and 4. 11-12 for attacks on sins of speech; also James 2. 1-7 and 5. 1-8 for his attitude toward wealth.
4. Examine 1 John 5. 6-8 in the *Revised Standard Version, The New English Bible,* and Phillips' translation and compare to the King James Version. The

famous Trinitarian passage is no longer included even in the margin, for no manuscripts from an early period contain it. This passage illustrates the necessity of using modern translations for Bible study.

5. Compare the table of duties in 1 Peter 2. 18 to 3. 7 with that in Colossians 3. 18 to 4. 1. Do you find any marked differences?

6. Compare 1 Peter 2. 13-17 with Romans 13. 1-7; one was probably written from Rome and the other to Rome. What bearing do these passages have on the modern problem of religion in a sovereign State?

7. Are any of the Catholic Epistles as valuable for study in a modern church school as Galatians? Formulate clearly the reasons for your opinion.

8. Is the *religious* value of any of the books affected by the conclusion taken toward authorship? Should a book be of less value because we do not know for certain the author's name? Why not?

CHAPTER TEN

THE DEFENSE OF THE FAITH

"WHAT is Christianity?" is a question to which a wide variety of answers has been given. The later Church had previous credal formulations to guide her, but the earliest believers had to answer the question for the first time. At the end of the first century there were wide differences in belief among those who looked to Jesus. This is not apparent to us because the only literature which has been preserved is that which a later Church deemed orthodox. Those labeled "false teachers" were doubtless just as certain that the epithet belonged more properly to their accusers. In the selection of her canon of Scripture, the Church as a whole was to distinguish between that which was true and that which was false teaching.

We noted in the last chapter something of the apologetic and argumentative character of the later books of the New Testament. We saw that First John was written in opposition to a view of Christ which would deny the reality of his fleshly existence. Most of the other teachings which were labeled false cannot be described so clearly. The reason is that they were condemned rather than refuted. It is unfortunate when differences of opinion are met by personal abuse rather than reasoned argument. In this chapter we shall review briefly the contents of Jude, Second Peter, and the Pastorals (First and Second Timothy and Titus) reserving most of our attention for the distinctive arguments of the Epistle to the Hebrews.

The little Epistle of Jude contains an especially virulent assault against certain false teachers. Its author regarded some who had gotten into the community as "stains on your religious meals" because their teaching led to immorality. In his attack Jude wove together an extraordinary number of allusions to Jewish lore, and even quoted from late Jewish books such as the apocalypse of Enoch. The readers are urged to "contend earnestly for the faith which was once for all delivered unto the saints" as they waited for "the mercy of our Lord Jesus Christ." The little Epistle is *a vigorous invective* but does not give us a very definite statement of what the correct faith is or where it might be found.

Apparently, however, the tract was effective in meeting the emergency, for it was quoted almost verbatim in our Second Peter. That Epistle came from a still later generation when other "false teachers" were to be combated. The particular occasion lay in the difficulty over *the delay in the coming of Christ*, which was causing many to lose faith. The answer which was given by this second-century "Peter" was twofold. Since the world had once been destroyed by a Flood, it might in the future be consumed by fire. Since a thousand years are but a day in the sight of the Lord, we should not interpret "soon" by our experience of time. When this pseudonymous author wrote, a collection of Pauline letters was in circulation "wherein are some things hard to be understood." Many modern readers will second that judgment.

Another name which was utilized in meeting the perils of this later time was that of Paul. Timothy and Titus had been his faithful coworkers in the missionary expansion of the Church. Such communities as Crete and Ephesus were now in need of fine Christian leaders, such as these had been. We do not learn much from these "Pastoral Epistles" about the duties of church officials. The author was not arguing for some particular form of church government. As always, men were more important than machinery. We are impressed chiefly by the fact that the moral requirements for the ministry were so elementary. These letters reveal the influx of former pagans, making the maintenance of high ethical standards, even among the leaders, extremely difficult.

The false teachings which are opposed had at least two characteristics; they dealt with *futile speculations*, and led to *ascetic practices*. We do not know enough about the period to identify them with any certainty. Opposed to these, "Timothy" and "Titus" are exhorted to maintain *"sound doctrine."* This body of beliefs is not set forth in detail, but the phrase reveals a striking difference from the real Paul. Faith is no longer the believing reception of God's redemption; it is a body of doctrine which is to be guarded intact. It is a deposit which is committed unto them, the "doctrine which is according to godliness."

These Epistles abound in phrases which appear to be drawn from current liturgies, such as "the King eternal, immortal, invisible, the only God." There are succinct confessions of faith which may be drawn from baptismal formulas. Snatches of early Christian hymns are quoted, and a series of "faithful sayings" current in the Church of the time. The Epistles contain many quotable aphorisms such as "Godliness with contentment is great gain." Their sober moralism is in many ways more congenial to the ecclesiastical mind than Paul's stress upon faith and the

Spirit.   Reflecting as they do the average Christianity of the beginning of the second century the Epistles remain useful manuals for the average church of every age.

The one canonical book from the postapostolic age which gives a reasoned defense of the faith is the Epistle to the Hebrews.   It is *the first Christian apologetic*. It was finally received into the canon on the claim that it had been written by Paul.   However, his name is not found in the book itself, and it is so different from the Pauline letters that the one certain conclusion about its authorship is that Paul did not write it.   Barnabas, Apollos, and Priscilla are among the many names which have been suggested.   Since we have no real information, however, speculation on the author's name is fruitless.

It is more important to know that he was *the most cultured literary artist* contributing to the New Testament.   He knew the Greek translation of the Old Testament thoroughly and quoted from it as authoritative.   His thought world had much in common with that of Philo, the Alexandrian Jew.   Despite the traditional name, the readers were certainly not Hebrews in the sense that they spoke that language.   In fact, there are indications that many of them at least were Gentiles rather than Jews.   But the author was not thinking of any distinctions of race.   He was writing to "Christians" whose sacred Scriptures were the Greek translation of the Old Testament.

The peril which the readers faced was not that they might return to Judaism, but that they would repudiate their faith entirely.   That danger was especially acute because they were now facing a new persecution. The author looked back on an earlier time when they had passed through a baptism of fire. Many scholars believe that these readers are to be found in Rome. This would account for the greetings from "those in Italy." In that case the earlier persecution might be the one under Nero, and the letter would be dated toward the close of the reign of Domitian (81-96).

The author sought to show by a reasoned argument that Christianity was the best religion. His method was to demonstrate its superiority over the next best, which was Judaism. For the author of the Epistle to the Hebrews, religion was primarily worship. Christianity is presented as the faith which *alone gives access to God.* To appreciate this little book the reader must make the mental effort to put himself back in the place of the original recipients. They had neither priests nor sacrifices nor temples. They were a humble group of people meeting in a modest dwelling. Their sacred book described an elaborate cultus, but they themselves had no ceremonies except a simple gathering for praise and thanksgiving, and a meal of bread and wine. Enthusiasm had grown cold, and it was the task of the author to arouse it anew by setting forth the majesty and finality of their faith.

The first section sets forth *a series of contrasts.* Jesus is presented as the bearer of a higher revelation than the angels who had mediated the Law. That was because he was the Eternal Son, who was the express image of the Father. Later the author appeals to such incidents in the human life of Jesus as his sharing in human temptation, and being made perfect through obedient suffering. But the proof which he offers for the superiority of the Son over the angels is derived from Old Testament Scripture, not from history. When the passages which he quotes are examined in their original context, we find that most of them have nothing to do with a Messiah. We must never forget that the author was working under presuppositions of his own time. Arguments are always for a day. The validity of our convictions fortunately is not dependent upon the adequacy of the apologetic which we are able to offer.

The next comparisons are with Moses and Aaron. Modern writers would compare Jesus with such figures as Confucius; Gautama, the Buddha; and Mohammed. There were no comparable figures in the Gentile religions of the Mediterranean world of that time. Though they knew lords many, such as Attis, Osiris, Mithras, and the like, no one claimed that these were historical characters such as Jesus of Nazareth. But the Jewish figures made an admirable foil to present the supremacy of Jesus. Moses had led the children of Israel into the land of Canaan, but this was not the promised rest of God. Aaron had established an elaborate priesthood, but it was not able to bring men actually into fellowship with God.

The heart of the argument lies in the contrast with Aaron. Jesus is presented as *the high-priest who offered himself as the one and complete sacrifice.* At first glance, this seems to us a curious perversion of history. While Jesus had not attacked the Jewish sacrificial system, he certainly did not place it in the foreground. As a layman he had no part in the ministry at the altar. He had not even belonged to the priestly tribe of Levi. But the author of Hebrews turned all of these points to his own case. Jesus had not been a priest on earth because his altar was in heaven. Though his physical descent did not qualify him to minister in the Temple at Jerusalem, Jesus

was of a higher order of ministry, the order of Mel-
chizedek.   The real point in appealing to this elusive
figure from the Old Testament lay in the insistence
that Jesus was a Priest in the right of his own person,
not because of physical descent.

Other New Testament writers had used the figure
of blood offerings as an analogy to the sacrifice of
Jesus on the cross.   But this author makes this comparison central.   He adds the thought that Jesus was
the Priest who presented the offering of his own blood
at the altar in heaven, as well as the victim who was
slain.   The many offerings by sinful men of the blood
of bulls and goats had not been able to cleanse the
consciences of men.   Now the self-offering of the sin-
less Son of God had brought the removal of sins, and a
new covenant relation with God whereby the veil of
separation was removed.

While the author was clearly absorbed by his subtle
arguments, his major objective did not lie in the realm
of theological speculation.   His real aim was *practical*.   Possibly he did not expect many to appreciate
his reasoning.   He did want to keep all from apostasy.
He warns them that there can be no second repentance for those who have once repudiated the faith.
This extreme position must be understood against
the background of the persecution.   Believers in
Christ could not fall away in time of danger, and
then expect to knock at the door of the Church and
receive forgiveness.   One of his most eloquent appeals
ends with the words, "Our God is a consuming fire."
The readers should be men of faith, who lived in the
consciousness of the unseen world and the coming salvation.   The best-known chapter in the Epistle is the
roll call of the ancient heroes of faith, who had been

steadfast in every difficulty even though they had not in their lifetime received the promise. The readers have also the inspiring figure of Jesus before them. He was not only the pioneer of their faith, but would soon bring the consummation of their salvation.

Despite its majestic insights, the Epistle to the Hebrews has not been an unmixed blessing. It is more responsible than any other book of the New Testament for the retention of the idea that a bloody sacrifice was necessary in order to make possible the forgiveness of men's sins. Jesus himself taught that the forgiveness of sins waited only upon the forgiving spirit in the heart of the petitioner. As a matter of fact, there was very little blood shed in the crucifixion. It is difficult to see how belief in the atoning efficacy of the blood can really be joined to the ethical religion of Jesus and the prophets. It is one of the thought forms which this author took for granted along with most of the men of his generation. It is a reminder of the fact that all arguments are in terms of the ideas of a particular age. An apologetic for our own day will be just as temporary. But this author had grasped something more than fallible human reasoning. Above all of the changing fashions of thought, "Jesus Christ is the same yesterday, and today, and forever."

BOOKS FOR FURTHER STUDY

William Barclay, *The Letters to the Hebrews.*
E. F. Scott, *The Pastoral Epistles* (Commentary on the Moffatt translation).

SUGGESTIONS FOR BIBLE STUDY

1. Compare Jude with 2 Peter 2 in order to verify the

dependence of the latter.   Note the picturesque figures of speech.

2. Read 1 Timothy 3. 1-13.   How adequate do you find the description of the qualifications for the ministry? Read 1 Timothy 5. 3-16 for its description of the care of Christian widows.   Was the aim simply charitable or to provide an order of church visitors?

3. Study 1 Timothy 6. 3-18 to verify the description of the Pastorals given in the text; what would Paul have thought of the idea that a person could be "rich in good works"?

4. Study 2 Timothy 3. 16, if possible with a commentary. This verse has occupied a prominent place in the discussion of Biblical inspiration.   The Revised Standard Version text is to be preferred.   The verse does not give a statement of the inspiration of Scripture, which no early Christian would have denied, but of the *uses* of such Scripture.   Many persons were refusing to use the Old Testament in the early 2nd Century A.D. So the writer emphasized the fact that *"all* scripture" is worthy.   Note in 1 Timothy 5. 18 that a word of Jesus is apparently cited as Scripture alongside of the Old Testament (Luke 10. 7) .

5. Turn to Jeremiah 31. 31ff. to see the original context of the New Covenant passage (Hebrews 8. 7-13) .   Is there anything in Jeremiah which states the necessity of a bloody death in order to inaugurate that covenant?   Note again in 10. 5-9 that the author turns the rejection of sacrifices in Psalms 40. 6f. simply into a rejection of the Levitical sacrifices.   Read Hebrews 9 for a statement of his idea of the sacrificial work of Jesus. In what different terms would you state your conviction that Jesus had brought perfect access to God?

6. How can the men and women named in Hebrews 11 be examples of Christian faith?   What difference in his use of the word "faith" from that in Paul?

7. Why should the Epistle to the Hebrews deny the possibility of a second repentance?   6. 4-6; 10. 26-31.

CHAPTER ELEVEN

THE TRIUMPH OF FAITH—REVELATION

THE book of Revelation has been the happy hunt-ing ground for many religious faddists. Those who are intensely preoccupied with its pages usually as-sume either that it contains a veiled prophecy of world history, or exact prediction concerning the end of the world. On the other hand, to many devout Christians it is a mysterious enigma, a book sealed with seven seals. They avoid it because they are revolted by its gruesome scenes, or frankly confess that they do not possess the key to the understanding of its strange imagery.

The only way in which we can come to a true com-prehension of this book is through some knowledge of the type of literature to which it belongs. One such *apocalypse* (the Greek word for "revelation") is in-cluded in our Old Testament, the book of Daniel. Jude quotes from Enoch, and still another is included in the Apocrypha under the name of Second Ezra. Under the form of visions and dreams of ancient worthies, later Jews wrote to hearten their discouraged contemporaries by proclaiming the certainty of God's triumph. Daniel appeared in the crisis of the perse-cution under Antiochus Epiphanes, beginning in 167 B. C. Second Ezra (also called Fourth Ezra) was writ-ten to encourage the Jews who had seen the fall of their holy city in 70 A. D. The books were "tracts for hard times," witnessing to invincible faith in the ulti-mate sovereignty of God, despite the calamities under which the righteous were then suffering.

The Revelation of John was not written under the name of some ancient worthy, for prophecy had revived in the early Christian Church. As early as the middle of the second century this prophet was supposed to have been John, the son of Zebedee. The book itself does not claim to come from an apostle. Many find it difficult to see how a writing which is so full of revenge could be a revelation of Jesus to one who had known him in the flesh. Others point out that this "son of thunder" had wanted to call down fire from heaven on an unreceptive Samaritan village. The interpretation of the book is not affected by our decision as to whether *the author* was one of the twelve apostles, or an unknown prophet by the name of John who had been exiled to the island of Patmos.

In any case the author wrote in the spirit and method of the Jewish apocalyptists who had preceded him. He was saturated with the imagery of such books as Zechariah, Ezekiel, Daniel, and Isaiah. Symbols from heathen astrology and mythology were also included, as in the sun goddess in chapter 12. No one should deny that John had had genuine visions. Every mystic sees his visions in terms of his previous spiritual background. It is highly probable that some earlier literary material was incorporated by the author. This was a frequent practice in the writing of such books. Nevertheless, the book as a whole is the product of a unitary conception. Knowing the literary custom of expanding such books of visions, John closed with terrible maledictions against anyone who might mutilate or expand his own revelation.

Revelation is one of the greatest pieces of *creative imagination* in world literature. To some readers this praise may seem to deny its character as actual revelation. But as one interpreter has said, "We must decide whether we are to look upon it as bad history and geography or good poetry." We should learn from the study of this book that revelation does not consist in supernaturally bestowed information about objects beyond sense experience, nor infallible predictions of future history. *Revelation concerns the purpose of God in his relation to the world.*

The crisis which called forth the book is mirrored in the letters to the seven churches—Ephesus, Smyrna, Pergamum, Thyatira, Sardis, Philadelphia, and Laodicea. They were the leading centers of Christian propaganda in the province of Asia, where the faith was then most strongly implanted. The letters reveal the internal peril of *false teachings* leading to immorality, a heresy which John labels the Nicolaitans. The other peril is that of *outward persecution*. According to ancient tradition, this came at the end of the reign of Domitian (81-96). Little evidence for such a persecution has been preserved, however, outside of the book of Revelation itself. Since individual martyrs are named, it is clear that as yet the persecution had not gone far. But the author envisaged a death struggle between the infant Church and the bestial empire which was committing the supreme blasphemy of calling for the worship of the emperor.

In the apocalyptic section (4. 1 to 21. 4), a terrible extension of that persecution is foreseen. The two mythical figures of the beast and the false prophet are given a veiled application to contemporary history. The beast, whose deathstroke has been healed, contains a reference to the Nero legend. After the death of this persecutor, the belief arose that he had not died but had gone to the East and would return at the head of the Parthian armies. When it was no longer possible to believe that he was alive, legend held that he would return from the dead. Hence, "the beast that thou sawest was, and is not; and is about to come up out of the abyss." Nero Caesar is one of the most popular solutions of the mysterious number, 666. However, the explanation may lie simply in the fact that three times it falls just short of the perfect number, seven. According to the same kind of numerical calculations, Jesus stood for 888, which was in each digit one more than the perfect number.

The false prophet had the task of making all peoples worship this incarnation of Antichrist. The imperial priesthood seems to have been in the author's mind. Those who did not worship the image of the beast were to be killed. Hence John writes, "Blessed are the dead who die in the Lord *from henceforth,*" for they would suffer a martyr death and go directly to the presence of God. While the peril of the Church had not yet reached this proportion, John saw clearly the inevitable antagonism. *Absolute loyalty to God could not be united with the acceptance of the complete sovereignty of a secular state which denied God's ultimate authority.* John used mythical symbols to encourage the Church. If the God-opposing powers were now so virulent on earth, it was because the dragon had already been cast down out of heaven. If the victory had been won there under the leadership of Michael, how much more certain was the victory of the Son of man on earth!

The apocalyptic section begins with an introductory vision of God sitting upon his throne surrounded by a heavenly chorus singing his praises. These heavenly cult scenes are scattered throughout the book

and present a welcome blissful relief from the pictures
of horror and bloodshed on earth. The imagery of
Oriental courts is drawn upon to portray the unpic-
turable splendor of God; but no attempt is made to
describe "the one sitting on the throne."

In all of the throng, no one is found worthy to
unseal the roll containing the world's destiny until
one comes who is described as both "the Lion of the
tribe of Judah" and the Lamb. He receives the worship of the heavenly host akin to that for God himself.
No book goes further in portraying the exalted Christ
as an object of worship. He is both the Lamb who
was slain from the foundation of the world, and the
Lamb who is King of kings and Lord of lords.

As the seals are opened at the beginning of chapter
6, a succession of *plagues* is let loose on earth. Four
horsemen bring in turn conquering war, strife, famine,
and pestilence. With the fifth seal, persecution is por-
trayed, and with the sixth a series of cosmic disasters.
While we wait breathlessly for the seventh, the author
interrupts his portrayal to recount in chapter 7 the
sealing of the saved community. This and the measur-
ing of the Temple in a later "intermezzo" signify the
preservation of the believers, not from physical harm,
but from spiritual disaster. To heighten the contrast,
a glorious picture is introduced at this point of the
redeemed who have "come out of *the* great tribution."
"They shall hunger no more, neither thirst any more;
neither shall the sun strike upon them, nor any heat.
. . . And God shall wipe away every tear from
their eyes."

The calamity introduced by the seventh seal is a set
of trumpets modeled in part after the plagues which
Moses brought upon Egypt. The last three trumpets

are identified as the three woes. Before the third woe, however, John makes his long digression introducing the figure of Antichrist under various aspects (chapters 10-14). The idea of an opponent of God in the end time had long been a part of Jewish expectations and contained elements ultimately derived from Babylonian and Persian mythology. The period of his domination was to be one-half of seven years, or 1,260 days. As we have already noted, John found the manifestation of the beast in the blasphemous claims of the Roman Empire.

The last woe introduces the seven bowls, a series of plagues which leads up to the final judgment upon evil. These disasters come to a climax in the fall of Babylon, symbolized by a harlot woman in contrast to the bride of Christ. John is clearly alluding to Rome, in contrast to the new Jerusalem. The Word of God leads the armies of heaven in victory. The beast and the false prophet and their worshipers are cast into the lake of fire and the dragon is chained in the abyss for one thousand years.

The idea of *a millennial reign of Christ* on earth has figured prominently in Christian thinking ever since John's apocalypse was accepted as authoritative for the Church. From the standpoint of the historical study of the Bible, the meaning of the passage is clear. A special prerogative is assigned to the martyrs who had been "beheaded for the testimony of Jesus," those who had not received the mark of the beast and hence had suffered death (20. 4-6). These would reign with Christ for a thousand years before the final onslaught of evil and the general resurrection and Judgment. If this prediction is taken literally, we must realize that the only way in which anyone could qualify for participation in the millennial reign would be by undergoing a martyr's death.   Historical students recognize that we have here John's adaptation of the current Jewish idea of a Messianic reign on earth preceding the final age to come.   In Fourth Ezra this period lasts four hundred years.   John does not have advance information as to God's timetable, but gives vivid expression to the faith that "Whosoever shall lose his life for my sake shall find it."

The practical interest of John must continually be borne in mind.   The pictures of the new Jerusalem coming down out of heaven, and the four-square city lighted only by the glory of God are not to be taken as revelations of celestial geography.   Here *triumphant faith speaks through current imagery*.   As all Christians of his time, John believed that the end of the age was near.   There would be seven kings; he was writing under the sixth, and the seventh would reign only a little while before the coming of Antichrist and the final drama.   "I come quickly" is the word which he hears, and John answers back in eager longing, "Come, Lord Jesus."

But in a world where the ruling political power was making such blasphemous demands, could the Church be kept faithful unto the end?   *The cowards* are named first among the sinners who should be cast into the lake that burned with fire and brimstone.   "Be thou faithful unto death, and I will give thee the crown of life. . . . He that overcometh, I will give to him to sit down with me in my throne."

Herein lies the great contemporary value of the book of Revelation.   We too live in a perilous hour when little hope for the triumph of right is to be seen on the immediate horizon.   The beast and the false

prophet are unleashed in the world with terrible fury.
There is every temptation to despair and compromise.
We cannot see the way out any more than could John,
but we too may be undergirded with the confident
faith that God is still the ultimate power, and his purpose will yet triumph. We do not believe as did John
that the end of the age is near. We do believe that
his revelation is valid, for *history does find its consummation in God.* It will yet be true that "The
kingdom of the world is become the kingdom of our
Lord, and of his Christ; and he shall reign for ever
and ever."

BOOKS FOR FURTHER STUDY

Charles M. Laymon, *The Book of Revelation.*
Julian P. Love, *1 John, 2 John, 3 John, Jude, and
Revelation,* vol. 25 in Layman's Bible Commentary.

SUGGESTIONS FOR THE STUDY OF REVELATION

1. Compare the situations in the churches of Ephesus (2.
   1-7), Pergamum (2. 12-17), and Laodicea (3. 14-22).
   When Ignatius wrote letters to churches in Asia Minor
   twenty years later he did not address either of the last
   two. Could you guess why?
2. Read the scenes of heavenly worship: 5. 9-14; 7. 12; 11.
   17-18; 14. 3; 15. 3-4; 19. 1-5. What do they reveal concerning the Christian liturgy of the time?
3. Why should the lamb have been used as a symbol for
   Jesus? Compare 5. 6-8; 14. 1-5; 17. 14.
4. Compare the series of woes in Revelation 6 with those
   in the apocalyptic passage in Mark 13. 7-9, 24-27. Compare also the series of trumpets in chapters 8 and 9 with
   the plagues in Exodus 7-11.
5. Compare the description of the Beast in chapter 13
   with that in chapter 17. A great deal of ingenuity has
   been spent in the attempt to identify the heads of the
   beasts with particular Roman emperors. The author,

however, is probably writing under the sixth emperor not because he has counted from some historical list but because he believed that he was that near the end of a series of seven.

6. Verify the fact that the millennial reign was only promised to the martyrs (20. 4-6). Notice that the apocalyptic section proper ends with 21. 4. The holy city in 21. 10 to 22. 5 is not meant to follow in point of time, but is an independent description of the new world. Note that it is not a heaven to which believers are to go at death, but a new age to follow the present age.

7. Do you think that the Jesus of Revelation bears much resemblance to the Jesus of the Gospels? Can both be true?

8. Do you find a spirit of vengeance dominant in Revelation? Does it despair of a victory of love and appeal in the end to force? What bearing does this have on the hopes which we cherish?

CHAPTER TWELVE

THE NEW TESTAMENT AND THE CHURCH

OUR survey of the circumstances under which the earliest Christian literature was written makes it clear that it was the Church which produced the New Testament. The religious life of later generations has been nourished by this fountain of inspiration. But these books did not produce that life in the first place. They are a *record* of the first creative experiences of those who found in Christ salvation from the ills of life, and their hope for the best which might come.

Christianity did not arise as a religion of a book in the sense that Mohammedanism began with the writing of the Koran, or Mormonism grew from the appearance of the Book of Mormon. The earliest Christians, of course, had the sacred writings of the Jews on which they might nourish their experience of God. But they read even these books from the standpoint of their new faith. Early Christianity was not a religion of a book in anything like the degree of the contemporary Judaism. The aim of the Jews was to produce commentaries on the Law. The Christians produced no commentaries on the words of Jesus for they were *possessors of the living Spirit of God*.

The earliest Christians proclaimed a word of God. The written word arose only in connection with the needs of preaching. First came the message of the flaming evangelists, the bearers of the good news. In fact, as we have seen, the first generation of believers did practically no writing. The most creative period

in the spread of the gospel was quite without the benefit of what we know as the New Testament. Experience is always primary; the record comes afterward,
and cannot produce the same glow except as it passes
through the quickening experience of another.

It follows that *the New Testament is the record of
the faith of the earliest Church.* That faith did not
consist in information about the life and teachings of
Jesus, but in a conviction about his ultimate significance for men. The Gospels were not written by
admirers of Jesus of Nazareth. Peter and Paul and
John had not proclaimed the superior ethics of a Galilean teacher, nor the God-consciousness which had
been attained by a village carpenter. The pages of
the New Testament were written to show men that
"God was in Christ reconciling the world unto himself." The writers were moved by the conviction that
"God so loved the world that he gave his only
Son, that whoever believes in him should not
perish but have eternal life." From the earliest
book to the latest, the same general message is
sounded forth. The early Christians were not concerned with the heroic martyrdom of an ancient Jew.
They sought to share their knowledge of a saving act
of God for all men. If the New Testament is to be
understood truly, it must be read with this purpose in
mind.

Not only were the individual writings in our New
Testament produced to meet the needs of the Church;
it was *the Church which selected these particular
books to be a standard for her teaching.* The authoritative writings came to be known as the canon of Scripture. They did not come to this eminence suddenly,
nor through any arbitrary decision. A long process

of sifting lay behind the ultimate canonization by con-
ciliar decision.   The official bodies pronounced authoritative what a long succession of leaders of the
Church had found to be most valuable in building up
the body of Christ.   The heart of the collection took
form toward the end of the second century when the
idea of a New Testament to stand beside the Old
Testament first found favor.   But agreement on about
ten of the borderline books was not reached for two
centuries more.   We can trace here only the barest
outline of this story.

Each of our Gospels was written in the expectation
that it would be *the* Gospel.   Others were composed,
such as the Gospel of Peter, the Gospel of Thomas, the
Gospel according to the Hebrews, and the Gospel according to the Egyptians.   However, none of these
ever received serious consideration for the canon.   At
first, some parts of the Church used one Gospel and
others another, but by the middle of the second century the idea of a fourfold Gospel had taken root.
Possibly it arose with the protagonists of the Gospel
according to John.   Fortunately, the attempt to weave
them together into a kind of harmony did not sup-
plant the idea of a fourfold Gospel.   Already in the
year 185, Irenaeus, Bishop of Lyons, could write, "It
is impossible that the Gospels should be in number
either more or fewer than these.   For since there are
four regions of the world wherein we are, and four
principal winds, and the Church is as seed sown in
the whole earth, and the Gospel is the Church's pillar
and ground, and the breath of life: it is natural that
it should have four pillars."

At this time, the Church was in great need of an
authoritative definition of its faith, because of a wide-

spread movement known as Gnosticism. This embraced Christians who had absorbed so many of the religious ideas of the Hellenistic world that it was felt by the main body of the Church that the distinctiveness of Christianity was threatened. At a somewhat earlier period (140) a teacher by the name of Marcion, who was pronounced heretical, had formed the first canon of New Testament Scripture. Since he rejected the Old Testament, he needed some written foundation for his branch of the Church. He edited a version of the Gospel according to Luke and ten of the Epistles of Paul. It is highly probable that the canon of the Catholic Church first arose to offset the collection which Marcion had made.

The slogan which was used in combating these false teachings was that of "*apostolic.*" The apostolic teaching was the true teaching. Two of the Gospels were believed to come directly from apostles and Mark and Luke from their disciples. But the gospel needed authoritative interpretation. Hence, the "apostle" should stand after the "Gospel." But of all of the apostles, only Paul had left any considerable body of writings. His letters had been collected for some time. Opposed to Marcion's collection of ten, the Catholic Church set a collection of thirteen (adding First and Second Timothy and Titus). But Paul was not one of the original Twelve. It was important to have an authoritative witness to his apostleship. The second book of Luke's history served this purpose admirably. It was given the title, "The Acts of the Apostles"; and became the connecting link between the two portions of the canon, the Gospel and the apostle. In its pages Paul stands beside Peter and John as the apostle *par excellence.*

The Church did not possess many other important writings for which apostolic authorship could seriously be maintained. First Peter and First John were generally accepted as canonical, and sometimes Jude and a second letter of John. The Epistles of Barnabas and Clement had wider usage at this time than any of the others which were ultimately accepted. The Epistle to the Hebrews had been known early in the West, but it was not looked upon as apostolic. Only gradually did the Alexandrian view that it was Pauline win acceptance. It should be realized that the Alexandrians did not really possess better tradition on this point. Accepting the authoritative character of its teaching, they had to ascribe it to an apostolic author. That is to be borne in mind concerning all of the "Catholic" Epistles. Their acceptance into the canon depended upon establishing an apostolic author. James and Second Peter first became serious candidates for acceptance in the middle of the third century. For a long time the number of General Epistles varied, but a determining influence was exercised by Bishop Athanasius when he wrote a letter in 367 A. D. commending exactly the seven which we have and no others.

Two other apocalypses were widely received in the Church at first, the Visions of Hermas and the Apocalypse of Peter. In the Eastern Church, the Apocalypse of John soon fell from favor also, and for a long time was not included in the canon. The West had the decisive voice at this point, but neither of the other two apocalypses retained authority after the second century. Here as elsewhere, the decision of the official church bodies only came afterward to ratify the practice which had grown up.

We have seen that the Church selected from its earliest literature a group of twenty-seven writings which should have an authoritative place beside the Jewish Scriptures which they inherited. It should be noted by all who are interested in the teaching work of the Church that without exception *these were books written for adult readers* and are concerned with adult experience. The Gospels have a few stories which concern children, such as the visit of the boy Jesus to the Temple at Jerusalem and the healing of the twelve-year-old daughter of Jairus. But it is very clear that the books themselves were not written for youthful readers. They record the incident of the bringing of little children to Jesus that he might touch them. But in the gospel tradition the actual children with whom Jesus dealt are quickly transformed into the "little ones" of the community. Mark and Matthew were thinking in terms of adult believers.

It is a striking fact that the New Testament contains so little about the religious training of children. The only words specifically directed to children in the entire New Testament are that they should obey their parents. The most direct guidance for the training of children is found in the words, "Ye fathers, provoke not your children to wrath: but nurture them in the chastening and admonition of the Lord." While many of the exhortations addressed to adults apply equally to youth, neither Paul nor any other New Testament writer was concerned with what we call Christian nurture. This does not surprise us when we remember that they expected the early end of the age. Nevertheless, it has a real bearing upon the use of the New Testament in the teaching work of the Church.

While the narrative portions of the New Testament can be read with interest at a relatively early age, the same is not the case with other parts. Such books as Second Corinthians, Ephesians, or Revelation will not be read by children with either understanding or great profit. That is recognized by all religious educators. All courses of study prepared for use in the elementary departments of the church school must pass such books by, no matter how fixed the endeavor may be to make the lessons Bible-centered. One of the unfortunate results of the idea of uniform lessons has been that such books as Romans and Hebrews could not be used for consecutive study in the church school. Obviously, they could never be adapted to the comprehension of children.

Though the books in our New Testament were originally written for adults, we face today the problem of the religious training of men and women from the cradle to the grave. It would be a very narrow view of Christian education to confine it simply to the study of the Bible. If we really believe that God is a living God, his revelation is not entirely confined to an ancient book. *A contemporary God* speaks in judgment and guiding influence through the life of today. Our problems must be faced directly through the experience of those who are called upon to meet them. It is a sound instinct which has guided educators to prepare courses for religious study based on contemporary life experiences of the age level of the students themselves.

Nevertheless, it is essential that the Bible should retain its *primacy in Christian education*. Our faith is not a vague general belief in God, nor are we to confuse the will of God with present-day American idealism. While contemporary experience should provide a confirmation of faith, it is not its foundation. Christian faith holds that a unique Word of God became flesh in Jesus. Here was an act of divine love for men which speaks more clearly than at any other point in history. Though Jesus found illustrations of God's grace in the world of nature, it is not characteristic of the New Testament to ground the love of God in an observation of natural phenomena. Belief in the love of God lay ultimately in his act for men in the life and death of Jesus of Nazareth. The distinctively Christian aspects of faith are not read from contemporary "life-situations" but are witnessed to us by the historic Christian revelation. A Christian analysis of life situations is to be made in the light of this revelation.

The centrality of the New Testament in Christian education does not determine the exact extent of Biblical material which may profitably be studied at any one age. At no age is a study made Christian simply by introducing it with a given number of verses from the Bible. Even for adults, the Bible does not always provide the best introduction to the Christian study of a given problem. We must remember that *a study is Christian when life is viewed in the light of our Christian faith.* The centrality of the New Testament in Christian education is determined not by the number of Biblical verses which are used. It is determined by the degree to which the light of the gospel is brought to bear upon a problem of life.

It is a mistake to take too narrowly practical a view of the use of the New Testament. As it arose to meet the needs of the Church of the first century, it will find a place in meeting the needs of the Church of today. But we should never forget that *the Bible is worth knowing for its own sake*. We would not think of reading a book of American history and stopping at the end of every page to ask what we had learned that we could put into immediate personal use. We read of the careers of Washington, Jefferson, and Lincoln because it is information that belongs to the equipment of every intelligent American. We are inspired thereby to go out and find how we can serve our country in our own generation.

In a similar way the New Testament is worth knowing for its own sake. It is the record of the religious heritage into which we have come. Its vocabulary is not always our vocabulary. New occasions teach new duties, and we find that final answers to all of our perplexing problems are not found written in any book. But we do find here the inspiring story of the beginnings of that movement to which we owe our own religious life. A study of its pages belongs to the education of anyone who has received from the heritage of Western civilization in which Christianity has been so influential. But to those of us who find here a word of God to men, this record is peculiarly sacred. It is an earthly vessel, as all that pertains to our humanity, but it contains the heavenly treasure. Here we read how "The Word became flesh and tabernacled among us," the word of God's grace and truth.

BOOKS FOR FURTHER STUDY

Floyd V. Filson, *Which Books Belong in the Bible?*
E. J. Goodspeed, *The Apostolic Fathers.*

QUESTIONS FOR MEDITATION AND DISCUSSION

1. In what sense is Christianity a book religion? Is it true that every high religion has its sacred literature, but no other religion has anything akin to the Church?
2. What are the best summaries which you know of the religious faith recorded in the New Testament? Do you know any clearer expressions of the nature of Christianity elsewhere?
3. Fragments of the gospels not included in the canon are printed in *The Apocryphal New Testament* by M. R. James. Other books not included in the canon may be found in various editions of *The Apostolic Fathers.* If accessible, read in some of the books referred to in the text. Do you think that it is unfortunate that any of them were left out of the canon? Are there any included which you would like to see dropped out?
4. Sometimes a plea is made for a larger Bible including later Christian writings down the centuries. Do you think that that would be advisable?
5. To what extent is the usefulness of the New Testament for children affected by its adult point of view? May this be offset by the use of a so-called "children's Bible"? What parts of the New Testament have you never had a chance to study in the church school?
6. Why do you think that the New Testament should be central in Christian education?
7. How can more people be interested in a deeper study of the Bible? Can this be done through a less strange format for the Bible, a genuinely modern translation, or through more Biblical preaching from the pulpit?
8. Is the Bible worth knowing "for its own sake," or only for some immediate contemporary objective?

DATE DUE

JUN 3 '65			
OCT 5 '65			
OCT 25 '65			
JAN 3 '66			
JUNE'66			
DEC 7 1970			
JUN 9 1972			
MT. UNION			
MAR 7 1974			
GAYLORD			PRINTED IN U.S.A.